TOM ROBBINS

Tom Robbins. Photograph © Carl Studna.

TOM ROBBINS

A Critical Companion

Catherine E. Hoyser
and Lorena Laura Stookey

CRITICAL COMPANIONS TO POPULAR
CONTEMPORARY WRITERS
Kathleen Gregory Klein, Series Editor

Greenwood Press
Westport, Connecticut • London

Library of Congress Cataloging-in-Publication Data

Hoyser, Catherine Elizabeth.
    Tom Robbins : a critical companion / Catherine Hoyser and Lorena
Laura Stookey.
        p.   cm.—(Critical companions to popular contemporary
writers, ISSN 1082–4979)
    Includes bibliographical references and index.
    ISBN 0–313–29418–6 (alk. paper)
    1. Robbins, Tom—Criticism and interpretation.   I. Stookey,
Lorena Laura.   II. Title.   III. Series.
PS3568.0233Z69   1997
813'.54—dc21   96–53851

British Library Cataloguing in Publication Data is available.

Library of Congress Catalog Card Number: 96–53851
ISBN: 0–313–29418–6
ISSN: 1082–4979

First published in 1997

Greenwood Press, 88 Post Road West, Westport, CT 06881
An imprint of Greenwood Publishing Group, Inc.

Printed in the United States of America

The paper used in this book complies with the
Permanent Paper Standard issued by the National
Information Standards Organization (Z39.48–1984).

10 9 8 7 6 5 4 3 2 1

To our parents:
Irving R. Hoyser and Margaret E. Russell Hoyser
and Jean L. Porter Benson

Contents

Series Foreword

The authors who appear in the series Critical Companions to Popular Contemporary Writers are all best-selling writers. They do not have only one successful novel, but a string of them. Fans, critics, and specialist readers eagerly anticipate their next book. For some, high cash advances and breakthrough sales figures are automatic; movie deals often follow. Some writers become household names, recognized by almost everyone.

But novels are read one by one. Each reader chooses to start and, more importantly, to finish a book because of what she or he finds there. The real test of a novel is in the satisfaction its readers experience. This series acknowledges the extraordinary involvement of readers and writers in creating a best-seller.

The authors included in this series were chosen by an Advisory Board composed of high school English teachers and high school and public librarians. They ranked a list of best-selling writers according to their popularity among different groups of readers. Writers in the top-ranked group who had not received book-length, academic literary analysis (or none in at least the past ten years) were chosen for the series. Because of this selection method, Critical Companions to Popular Contemporary Writers meets a need that is not addressed elsewhere.

The volumes in the series are written by scholars with particular expertise in analyzing popular fiction. These specialists add an academic focus to the popular success that the best-selling writers already enjoy.

The series is designed to appeal to a wide range of readers. The general reading public will find explanations for the appeal of these well-known writers. Fans will find biographical and fictional questions answered. Students will find literary analysis, discussions of fictional genres, carefully organized introductions to new ways of reading the novels, and bibliographies for additional research. Students will also be able to apply what they have learned from this book to their readings of future novels by these best-selling writers.

Each volume begins with a biographical chapter drawing on published information, autobiographies or memoirs, prior interviews, and, in some cases, interviews given especially for this series. A chapter on literary history and genres describes how the author's work fits into a larger literary context. The following chapters analyze the writer's most important, most popular, and most recent novels in detail. Each chapter focuses on a single novel. This approach, suggested by the Advisory Board as the most useful to student research, allows for an in-depth analysis of the writer's fiction. Close and careful readings with numerous examples show readers exactly how the novels work. These chapters are organized around three central elements: plot development (how the story line moves forward), character development (what the reader knows about the important figures), and theme (the significant ideas of the novel). Chapters may also include sections on generic conventions (how the novel is similar to or different from others in its same category of science fiction, fantasy, thriller, etc.), narrative point of view (who tells the story and how), symbols and literary language, and historical or social context. Each chapter ends with an ''alternative reading'' of the novel. The volume concludes with a primary and secondary bibliography, including reviews.

The Alternative Readings are a unique feature of this series. By demonstrating a particular way of reading each novel, they provide a clear example of how a specific perspective can reveal important aspects of the book. In each alternative reading section, one contemporary literary theory—such as feminist criticism, Marxism, new historicism, deconstruction, or Jungian psychological critique—is defined in brief, easily comprehensible language. That definition is then applied to the novel to highlight specific features that might go unnoticed or be understood differently in a more general reading of the novel. Each volume defines two or three specific theories, making them part of the reader's understanding of how diverse meanings may be constructed from a single novel.

Taken collectively, the volumes in the Critical Companions to Popular

Contemporary Writers series provide a wide-ranging investigation of the complexities of current best-selling fiction. By treating these novels seriously as both literary works and publishing successes, the series demonstrates the potential of popular literature in contemporary culture.

Kathleen Gregory Klein
Southern Connecticut State University

Acknowledgments

Every project of this nature involves help from several people. My gratitude extends to Tom Robbins, who generously granted interviews, information, and access to his friends and family. I also wish to thank Alexa Robbins, Fleetwood Star Robbins, Ruby Montana, Caylin Dougherty, Randy Sue Coburn, Carl Studna, and Stuart Applebaum. Special thanks to Kathleen Klein, Barbara Rader of Greenwood Press, and Lorena Stookey for their patience and support. The students of perhaps the first-ever Tom Robbins seminar earn my affection and respect for their intellectual curiosity. Library help came from Catherine Posteraro, Kathy Kelley, Linda Geffner at Saint Joseph College, West Hartford, Connecticut, and the staff of the Seattle Public Library. Bonnie Merk-Berman and Sr. Dorothy O'Dwyer helped with the manuscript typing. The Faculty Development Committee of Saint Joseph College provided funds which enabled me to interview Tom Robbins. This book is better because of those opportunities. Moral support came from Catherine Posteraro, Lenore Grubinger, D. Gwyn Crawford, Shyamala Raman, and the espresso bar gang at Borders Books, Manchester, Connecticut. Any inaccuracies are solely my responsibility.

Catherine E. Hoyser

It was a singular pleasure to encounter the likes of Q-Jo Huffington, the Great God Pan, and the Daughters of the Daily Special within the pages of Tom Robbins's books. I thank Robbins—and all of the honorary "Daughters" who contributed to this project.

Lorena Laura Stookey

TOM ROBBINS

The Life of Tom Robbins

At five years old, Thomas Eugene Robbins was dictating stories to his mother and protesting vehemently if she dared change a word (Strelow 97). This early sense of the importance of precise language makes it unsurprising that he became a writer. Robbins still labors intensely on finding the exact combination of words to convey his ideas. Once he writes the words on a page, few will change during the subsequent editing. "The reason I write so slowly is because I try never to leave a sentence until it's as perfect as I can make it. . . . So there isn't a word in any of my books that hasn't been gone over 40 times" (Egan, "Perfect" C9). When composing a text, Robbins works in his studio from 10:00 A.M. until 3:00 or so in the afternoon. The closer he is to the end of a novel, the shorter his work day becomes because of the sheer physical exhaustion of his writing process (Interview 1994; Edlin 42).

Contrary to the image some followers have of Tom Robbins, he is not a drugged-out comedian clinging to the 1960s. Robbins is intensely serious about writing, life, and creativity. His active imagination keeps him from becoming dismayed by the acuity with which he contemplates the world. Playfulness and wit rescue the earnest philosopher from depression over humanity's inhumanity. Joy is his means of survival. One girlfriend once told him that "the trouble with you, Tom, is you have too much fun" (Rogers 68). A self-described shy person, Robbins claims he cannot express himself well orally. Indeed, many of his responses to questions from book tour audiences seem practiced for the predictable questions he may receive. They are repeated when the same question comes up in a different venue. Many of his comments come from his novels.

Robbins produces a novel about every five years, following a general schedule of pleasure travel and recuperation for the first year after the book tours are finished. He spends the next four years researching, writing, editing, and attending to production processes for the next book (Interview 1994). He has published six novels, the most recent *Half Asleep in Frog Pajamas* (1994). To recuperate from that novel he visited Thailand and Burma, riding elephants through the bush for a month. The trip was a delayed honeymoon for him and his fourth wife, Alexa d'Avalon, another wildlife lover (Letter to author, 26 June 1995). Together for over ten years, they married in Bradenton, Florida, on March 17, 1994.

Robbins has written and read intensively since he was claimed by the writing muse at five years old. His first stories, recorded in a gift of a *Snow White and the Seven Dwarfs* scrapbook, were followed by continuous writing experiments. One of the stories in the *Snow White* scrapbook featured a pilot who, after crashing on a desert island, is taught to eat sand by a brown cow with yellow spots. Robbins jokes that his early ideas would fit with the fantasy in his novels (Rogers 70). He has described his youthful efforts as several attempts at novel writing with partial manuscripts abandoned. He began his professional writing career as a journalist, eventually writing art reviews for the two Seattle newspapers. He still writes articles for *Esquire* and other magazines.

Robbins's first novel, *Another Roadside Attraction*, published in 1971, is set against a backdrop of the 1960s subculture. The primary plot device is the stealing of the corpse of Jesus Christ from the catacombs beneath the Vatican. *Even Cowgirls Get the Blues* (1976) portrays the explorations of Sissy Hankshaw, a legendary hitchhiker and beautiful model with oversized thumbs. Robbins's third novel, *Still Life with Woodpecker* (1980), solidified his reputation as a writer of best-sellers. *Woodpecker* focuses on two characters with opposing philosophies of life. *Jitterbug Perfume* (1984) focuses on Alobar, who begins the novel as a medieval king and lives a thousand years, ending up as the janitor in Albert Einstein's lab. A parallel story line involves three people searching for the base note of a perfume that Alobar and his life's love, Kudra, developed. In 1990 Robbins's most overtly political novel was published. *Skinny Legs and All* tackles the Arab-Israeli conflict, Christian fundamentalism, and the conflict between commercialism and art. Perhaps the most fantastical of his novels, *Skinny Legs* includes inanimate objects as characters. The spoon, conch shell, can of beans, stick, and sock journey across the United States on the path to Jerusalem in honor of the ancient goddess Astarte and the biblical Jezebel. Art unites all of the story lines. Robbins's latest novel, *Half Asleep in Frog Pajamas* (1994), continues with a critique of greed and a concern for the future of the planet. A stock market crash such as the one in October 1987 places protagonist Gwen, a young stockbroker, in a desperate situation. She believes only an outlaw ex-stockbroker genius can save her career.

As it has from his early childhood writing, fantasy plays a major role in Robbins's texts, and his childhood environment could easily set the stage for his vivid imagination. He was born on July 22, 1936, in Blowing Rock, North Carolina. He has described the place as "an isolated, Appalachian village of tremendous natural beauty . . . whose economic backbone was tourism in summer and picking up empty beer bottles in winter." (Edlin 41). Every June, Blowing Rock would change from a depressed hillbilly town to a glamorous resort, inhabited by the rich and famous, who shopped in expensive boutiques run by entrepreneurs from Palm Beach, Florida, and Paris. The glamour of the visitors and, later, the glitz of the circus (with which he fell in love the first time he saw one at age four or five) became elements in his novels, which include characters, places, and objects that transform or disguise themselves, hiding behind masks, literally, or behind language by adapting phony accents and personas to match them. It is no surprise that Robbins spent several summers hanging around a circus, absorbing the ability of people to contort and distort themselves and create illusions (Interview 1995). He learned the truths behind the facades of the show. "I think maybe the carnival—the kind they had in the rural south—and the circuses were really the last vestiges of pagan celebrations. A dull, boring, vacant lot would suddenly fill with these strange people, and tents and banners and flags, and that night it would light up with neon. It was a magical transformation, and I loved it" (Rogers 69). The magic that he watched in the circus as a boy inhabits his novels. He has said that "I have always been a romantic—one of those people who believes that a woman in pink circus tights contains all the secrets of the universe" (Whitmer 54; Egan C1). He collects sideshow banners advertising freaks, geeks, and reptiles and owns a house in Florida near the winter headquarters of several circuses.

Another influence on Robbins must have been his mother, Katherine Robinson Robbins. The daughter of a Baptist minister, she wrote children's stories for religious magazines and was, as Robbins once described her, "a frustrated writer" (Edlin 41). She would interrupt her household tasks to take Robbins's dictations when the five-year-old was inspired; she lived until 1993. His father, also the child of a Baptist minister, was a utility company executive who, according to his son, "loved books." Robbins was the first of their four children and had one younger sister who died at four years of age; Tom was then seven. To the child Tom, bliss was his parents reading aloud to him (Strelow 97). But he also taught himself to read at age five, the same year he began his dictation of stories. He also said that by age four he "loved everything about books—the smell, size, weight, appearance" (Strelow 97). In fact, books "were a magic carpet for me" (Edlin 41). Asked how he got started as a novelist, he responded, "I started before I was old enough to know any better. My muse was a cradle-robber, a child-molester. She seduced an innocent, blue-eyed, tow-headed, pre-literate tot and turned him into a paragraph junkie" (Strelow 97).

In Warsaw, Virginia, where his family had moved in the forties, Robbins disguised his literary penchant during high school as he dated cheerleaders, played basketball, and became known as a sociable show-off and rebel (*Current Biography* 494). Reading was not the proper pursuit of a "real boy" of the South, so Robbins hid that side of himself while secretly reading "voraciously" (*Current Biography* 494). His rebelliousness earned a suspension from high school, and as a result his parents sent him to Hargrave Military Academy. He left Washington and Lee University in dishonor, after expulsion from his fraternity for a food fight that involved bombarding the housemother with biscuits. Robbins says that after the fraternity episode, "It finally became apparent that I didn't have the makings of a southern gentleman" (Rogers 68). Perhaps "southern gentleman" would not describe Tom Robbins at that time, although self-denigration and understatement are part of his repertoire. He is very much a considerate gentleman who looks fabulous in tails (see his appearance in the whorehouse scene of the movie *Mrs. Parker and the Vicious Circle* [1994]) and speaks with a dignified Virginia accent. No longer the gregarious high schooler, he is shy and reclusive, a person who warms up slowly to a person or group. At book signings and lectures, however, he talks with readers and fields questions with ease and aplomb, possibly with reliance on his pretour studies. He is a loyal friend to female and male alike, though he has more female friends than male; but his male friendships are extremely close. As with his writing, his friendships reflect quality rather than quantity.

After a two-year sojourn at Washington and Lee University in Lexington, Virginia, Robbins hitchhiked around the United States for a year. He has described thumbing as "a revelation" (Edlin 42). Further, he claims that he "had always dreamed of travel, but I came from a family with no sense of mobility" (Edlin 42). New York City was Robbins's first goal. He briefly entertained notions of becoming a poet and headed for the center of poetry in 1956. Shortly thereafter, he received his draft notice and, not wanting to carry a gun, joined the air force. The military, an unlikely choice for a free-spirited young man, proved unable to quench his ongoing rebelliousness. He taught meteorology to the South Korean Air Force, a rather uninspiring occupation since this air force flew regardless of the weather. Soon, he claims, he set up a black-market business selling toiletries which he discovered later went primarily to the Communist Chinese. He quips that he supplied Mao Tse-tung with Colgate for thirteen months (Edlin 42).

After the air force, Robbins returned to Virginia to study at the Richmond Professional Institute, now Virginia Commonwealth University. He graduated from the art, drama, and music institute with academic honors and a grade-point average of 3.7 in 1960 (*Current Biography* 495). While still in school, Robbins then started work at the Richmond *Times-Dispatch*. The conservative newspaper, which had an official policy forbidding photographs of blacks, did not appreciate his liberal views. Its editors were particularly outraged when he included in a music column a photograph of Sammy Davis, Jr., who had recently married Scandinavian actress Mai Britt. It had been serious enough when he inserted a photograph of the extraordinary trumpeter Louis Armstrong, but the racial climate of the early 1960s United States, especially the southern tier, did not support black-white couples. Robbins decided to leave Virginia to travel as far away as he could and still be in the continental United States. So in 1962 Robbins moved to Seattle, where he writes and occasionally paints and exhibits.

Not all the time in Richmond, however, was negative for Robbins. Beyond making a strong academic performance, he became friends with Mary Lou Davis, a woman who had been a friend of some of the major American artists in the peak of the Greenwich Village art days, and a group of artists who defied the conservative narrow-mindedness of Richmond. His first performance art appearance occurred when Davis, B. K. Kendrick, and Robbins painted their rear ends red. They climbed naked up on the rafters of a carriage house art studio while a friend charged admission, and this avant-garde display was one of many of their commentaries about the Richmond scene (Matera). In Seattle, Robbins performed a piece he called "Low-calorie Human Sacrifice to the Godless Minnie Mouse," after which he was arrested but not booked. He also performed "Stronger Than Dirt," which created such a scandal that Lloyd Clooney (the president of a Seattle television station) did "an outraged editorial about it on KIRO" (O'Connell 273). The friendship of Robbins, Davis, and Kendrick continues long-distance and is an example of the strong relationships Robbins, who is nonjudgmental and supportive, can have. Davis was studying to be a nurse when she was introduced to Kendrick, the painter; Bill Jones; and Robbins. She says that they helped her appreciate life on the edge. She claims that "Bill and Tom saved me from mediocrity" (Matera 9). She dropped her nursing plans, vowing to avoid the 9:00 to 5:00 workforce. Kendrick needed a model and a babysitter, and Davis moved in to serve as both. In the meantime, Kendrick and his wife divorced. Davis got pregnant and was abandoned by her child's father, whereupon Robbins and Kendrick stepped in as birth coaches and supporters during Davis's pregnancy. She says they went with her to her checkups and when asked at the hospital who was the father, both announced that they were. Davis declares that she was never intimately involved with Robbins or Jones, although she was briefly married to Kendrick. The three, as she recalls it, simply shared the house. Davis became deeply involved with drugs, and Robbins several times rushed her to the hospital from overdoses or accidents. Their friendships have survived all the vicissitudes of their lives. Davis recovered from her drug addictions. Robbins dedicated his first novel, *Another Roadside Attraction*, to her former husband, Kendrick. Most recently Robbins called on Davis for help during the filming of his novel *Even Cowgirls Get the Blues*. Uma Thurman wanted to master an authentic Richmond accent, so Robbins asked Davis to record some dialogue. Davis and her daughter from an earlier relationship (the illegitimate child was adopted by a wealthy Jewish couple) read portions of *Cowgirls* into a tape recorder and conversed in Richmond accents to help out the actress.

Robbins met his first wife, Susan, in Richmond. It was 1961. In an interview (1994), Robbins elaborately described the circumstances leading to their marriage. He was madly in love with a Jewish woman who hid their relationship from her family. To satisfy her conservative parents, she openly dated an appropriately Jewish boy. Robbins finally realized that she would never have the courage to defy her family and marry him. That disappointment, coupled with a hot argument over a lease with a rental agency, landed him in a bar across the street from the financial district, cooling off with a beer or two. A Richmond woman from one of the fine southern aristocratic families, Susan liked to go slumming by attending readings at coffeehouses. Robbins describes her as caught between Richmond high society and the allure of bohemian art life. Although Robbins had never formally met her, she was tall and blond and quite noticeable; so when she walked out in the middle of Robbins's poetry reading one night, the snub was unmistakable. Robbins was enraged by her rudeness and her superior attitude. When she walked into the bar where he was drowning his sorrows (she worked for a brokerage house across the street), he grabbed the opportunity to attack her rudeness and her insensitivity. Purged of his anger, Robbins waited for her response. She looked at him and asked, "Will you marry me?" They married in North Carolina, where no waiting period or blood test was required, the next morning. She and Kendall, her two-and-a-half-year-old-daughter from a previous marriage, accompanied Robbins to Seattle after a much heated argument. She did not want to leave Richmond, which except for its conservative and racist attitudes, he also loved. But intrigued by the painting of Mark Tobey and Morris Graves, he felt pulled to the rainforest of the northwest coast. He "was intrigued about what kind of landscape could produce a school of mystic painters" (Rogers 69). He also claims that intuition steered him to Seattle (O'Connell 272).

Robbins describes this marriage as lasting a few months; it lasted longer but did not survive. He writes that "It was less a marriage, in fact, than a performance piece. It was theatre. Living satire" (Letter to author, 28 July 1995). His wife moved out, leaving her daughter with Robbins. He became a single stepfather, glorying in taking the girl to all the art openings, operas, and plays that he reviewed for the *Seattle Times*. He would dress her in frilly dresses and pop her onto his motorcycle and zoom across town, a vision of gleaming metal, leather, and lace as they drove up to the art scene. After nine months she reunited with her mother, but Robbins is still close to her.

Robbins has given up the motorcycle riding he did with his stepdaughter and friends though his fondness for bikes is still evident. His favorite bike, and his last, was his BMW (Interview 1994). While excavating the space on which he built the writing studio and bedroom extension to his century-old house in La Conner, Washington, Robbins found a rust-encrusted toy cast-iron motorcycle. Years earlier, a friend had found an identical cast-iron bike encrusted in sand and rust while clam digging on a Seattle beach and had given the toy to Robbins (Interview 1994). These discoveries led to Robbins's extensive collection of 1950s tin toys. At the time few people collected these Japanese toys because they seemed common and were Japanese and, therefore, considered inferior. Since then these tin toys have become a collecting rage, pricing them out of Robbins's budget. He is happy with the seventy or more he does have, and they decorate the edges of his writing room. One of his toys has the word "Marx" on the side. Perhaps Marx Marvelous from his first novel, *Another Roadside Attraction*, owes part of his name to this tin motorbike, not just to the German political and economic theorist.

Robbins's attraction to these tin toys became the means through which he met Ruby Montana, famed collector and seller of 1950s memorabilia. Her store, Ruby Montana's Pinto Pony, is such a tourist attraction that it is featured on the Tourist Bureau Map of Seattle. Television shows, among them the 1980s–90s *Northern Exposure*, and movie personnel often rent items from her collections. Their favorite object is Smokey Judy, a full-size standing mount of a great brown bear that someone found and donated to Ruby's collection. When *House and Garden Magazine* approached Montana asking her permission to feature her store and collections, Montana requested that the magazine engage only Robbins for the piece (Interview 1994). It did. His article on Montana describes her, the store, and her collections in a way that shows his genuine admiration. Montana regularly recruits Robbins to be judge in the Ruby Montana Pinto Pony's Annual Spam Carving Contest, a fund-raiser for a Seattle food bank. A vegetarian, Montana started the project as an attraction for the store. Ironically the Hormel Meat Company, makers of Spam, exploited the idea for the first contest and launched a media campaign extolling the pink meat product. Not one to waste anything, Montana donates the carved Spam to the lions at the zoo but voices doubts that it is fit for animal consumption, let alone human (Interview 1994).

In addition to judging Spam contests and collecting toys, Robbins's activities include pursuing an interest possibly piqued by his air force duty in South Korea. Studying Eastern philosophy at the University of Washington marked a formalization of an avocation that Robbins still maintains. His interest in mysticism inspired his taking these classes when he first arrived in Seattle. Today he declares that the magazine/journal *Triangle*, a Buddhist review, is his favorite periodical (Interview 1994). This is saying a lot, since Robbins is something of a magazine buff, subscribing to about thirty publications (Interview 1994). Dressed in a satin smoking jacket and smoking a Cuban cigar, Robbins spends his Thursday evenings surveying his week's collection of journals. Sometimes his reading plants a kernel of an idea in his imagination that he then pursues as part of a writing project. This process began his research into the Sirius constellation and the Bozo and the Dogon peoples of Africa which he used in *Half Asleep in Frog Pajamas*, his latest novel (Interview 1994).

Robbins states that the keys to understanding his writing are a knowledge of the Tibetan Buddhist concept "crazy wisdom" and Greek myth (Interview 1995; letter to author, enclosure, 15 March 1995: McCaffery and Gregory 226). Influential in his study of mysticism and spirituality is the life work of the scholar and writer Joseph Campbell. Campbell is famous for his massive and detailed comparisons of Western and Eastern spirituality, myth, and belief. Robbins did a study tour of Mexican and Central American ceremonial sites with Campbell as leader. Each day the group toured a location such as the Mayan ruins of Chichén Itzá. In the evening, Campbell would talk to the group about what they had seen and experienced during the day. In a tribute upon Campbell's death, Robbins wrote that "Joseph Campbell was so conversant with the world of wonders that he awakened the potential for wonder in everyone he touched. He unbuttoned the secret earth for us and let the inexhaustible inspiration of Being stream through" ("Obituary" Sept./Oct. 1988: 98).

His admiration of Campbell's ability to unlock the earth's secrets for others gives an indication of Robbins's desire to embrace mind-expanding experiences. While he studied Eastern philosophy and worked for the *Times*, Robbins began experimenting with psychedelic drugs. In 1963, six months after his first LSD experience, he called in "well" to his editor at the *Times*, explaining that prior to this time he had actually been ill and, now that he was well, he would be staying at home (*Current Biography* 495). Robbins was among the earliest in the country to take LSD and other psychedelics. In 1964, looking for a community of like-minded experimenters he moved to New York. He did not find community, but he did have his first encounter with Timothy Leary, pioneer of psychedelic experimentation, during that stay. He and Leary were standing at a vegetable stand, and Leary asked Robbins "how to tell which brussels sprouts were good." Robbins, who had just attended a lecture by Leary at Cooper Union, responded that it was best to choose the ones that were smiling (Whitmer 54).

Years later the two met again as Robbins did a book signing at Papa Bach's in Los Angeles (Interview 1994). By then Leary knew of Robbins from his novels and articles. The younger man was, in fact, deluged by people wanting his autograph on their copies of *Still Life with Woodpecker*, his third novel, and the signing took four hours. The bookstore was too small for the crowd, so Robbins was set up to sign in an alley beside the store, seated at a low child's table. Autograph requesters had to kneel at the table to be able to speak with Robbins and make their requests. Leary happened by and instead of joining the crowd, joined a group of Mexicans that had gathered in a parking lot next to the alley, behind a chain-link fence. Leary enjoyed the scene of worshipers kneeling in front of Robbins as much as the puzzled Mexicans did. With hand signals, the two writers made plans to meet after the signing ended (Interview 1994). They were close friends until Leary's death in 1996.

Drugs were not necessarily an escape from reality for the early partakers, but rather a 1960s and 1970s effort at mind expansion. There are always those people, of course, who use drugs to escape responsibility. For Robbins, however, the drug experiments were adventures into his mind and into new perspectives. Robbins explains the influence that taking psychedelics had on his creativity and perspective: "Mainly, psychedelics left me less rigid, intellectually and emotionally . . . The borderlines between so-called reality and so-called fantasy, between dream and wakefulness, animate and inanimate were no longer as distinct, and I made some use of this newfound mobility in my writing" (McCaffery and Gregory 231). The eating of psychedelic mushrooms in *Another Roadside Attraction*, Robbins's first book, provides the characters with deeper connections to nature and a peace within themselves. In *Even Cowgirls Get the Blues*, the leader of the alienated rebel cowgirls eats peyote buttons in order to receive insights from the Mother Goddess. Her final vision leads her to understand that armed resistance against the male establishment was wrong because it perpetuated disharmony. In addition it was behaving with a negative male aggression that lowered the cowgirls to the level of masculine destructiveness. In later novels, marijuana smoking provides relaxation and, most importantly, a fresh perspective for many characters. None of Robbins's characters use hardcore addictive and destructive drugs such as crack cocaine or heroin. Cocaine is used in *Still Life*, but Robbins now somewhat regrets it (O'Connell 275; Interview 1995).

Robbins returned to Seattle after a year in New York and began writing an art column for the magazine *Seattle*. His fame in Seattle thus preceded his novel publications. Besides working for *Seattle* he hosted a radio show on KRAB 107.7, an "overground trans-conscious radio" station. He also

wrote articles for an underground newspaper, the *Helix*. Robbins reviewed the Doors' appearance at the Seattle Eagles Auditorium. The review's opening line is: "On July 23 and 24, the Eagles Auditorium was
raped and pillaged by the Doors" (*Helix* 1, 8 [July 25, 1967]: 11). It continues with high praise for the band and its musicians. The closing paragraph
declares, "The Doors are carnivores in a land of musical vegetarians. Their
craftsmanship is all the more astonishing in the light of their savagery.
They have the ensemble tightness of the Julliard String Quartet—but their
grandeur is not of the intellect but of warm red blood."

Another Robbins entry in the *Helix* features a rubbing of a dime under a
piece of paper and the declaration "The Dime That Called Picasso" ("My
Life" 10). The article is titled "My Life with Picasso." Robbins was drinking with his friends at their usual hangout, the Blue Moon, the first bar just
over the line from the alcohol-free zone of the University of Washington.
In the guidebook *Seattle Access*, writer-journalist Timothy Egan recom-
mends the Blue Moon and includes a Robbins Picasso story: "In his mind"
rather than out of it, as Robbins says, he made a collect call to Pablo Picasso (Interview 1994). Certain that Picasso was on the other end of the
line when his call went through, he waited for a chance to speak with the
master. The charges were refused by a voice Robbins describes as "gentle
and smooth, like paint squeezed fresh from a tube. I thought of cobalt
blue." His image of Picasso is of the artist in a petticoat and an African
mask; this figure of a man in a mask would appear in the novel *Jitterbug
Perfume*. The Blue Moon continues in business today and attests to its role
in the community by photographs, books, and wall paintings honoring the
tavern's life as a mecca for professors, graduate students, artists, and bik-
ers. Robbins claims that several books, poems, and plays have been written at the Blue Moon. He says that the FBI monitored the tavern because of
worry about the socialists and communists who assembled there. They
dropped the surveillance after forty years when they realized that the first
branch of the Communist Party in Seattle was not going to create revolu-
tion (Interview 1995). Robbins's notoriety has continued to become part of
popular legend in Seattle, as has his reputation as a good person who par-
ticipates in charitable and arts fund-raising. High society and the University of Washington basically ignore Robbins. He has read only once at the
university, when a student group invited him. On that occasion the large
concert hall was standing room only and many people had to be turned
away (Interview 1995).

As he resumed life in Seattle, Robbins began speculating about what
might happen if people were to discover that Christ had not actually

been divine. What if, instead of ascending into heaven, Christ had been merely a great man whose mummified corpse was hidden by the Catholic hierarchy in catacombs beneath the Vatican? Robbins began studying the history of early Christianity in preparation for developing the idea into a novel. He said he was a virtual walking encyclopedia on Jesus and the early Christian era (Interview 1995). In 1968 Robbins was invited to meet with Luther Nichols, West Coast editor of Doubleday Books, who praised his art columns and asked him if he would like to write a book on West Coast artists. Robbins took the opportunity to sell his novel idea, saying that the manuscript was still quite rough. Robbins left the coffee shop of the Benjamin Franklin Hotel (now a Westin), went home, and immediately started writing (O'Connell 265). The first year was difficult because his art world work and ties kept him from the novel. He left Seattle and settled with a girlfriend in South Bend, Washington. They first moved into a storefront for eight dollars a month rent and ate leftovers from the seafood restaurant where the young woman worked. On weekends he worked at the *Seattle Post-Intelligencer*. Two years later Robbins finished the novel.

The editors at Doubleday, some of whom were disturbed by the novel's portrayal of the Church, spent some time arguing over the novel's merits before finally deciding to publish it. Robbins took his $2,500 advance, converted it into yen, and bought a ticket to Japan (Interview 1994). Thus began the Robbins work pattern: one year to travel, three years to write, and one year for editing and publicity tours.

Another Roadside Attraction is an insider's view of the 1960s. In 1971 Doubleday published 6,000 copies in hardcover. Over seven years it sold slowly, advanced by word of mouth. When Lenore Fleischer, editor at Ballantine Books, bought the paperback rights for $3,500 in 1972 and issued the novel in paperback, sales increased considerably. In 1978 Robbins said, regarding sales of *Another Roadside Attraction*, "I made more in royalties in the last six months than during the previous seven years combined" (Edlin 41). By the late 1970s approximately 700,000 copies of the novel had been sold.

Reviewers were positive about *Another Roadside Attraction*. The British novelist Graham Greene praised Robbins's work. Auberon Waugh gave strong praise to Robbins as well, calling him "the best of the Californian writers" (366) (apparently the sixties are epitomized by California for the British). College and high school students appreciated the novel's fantasy and humor and probably the relaxed attitude about sex. Praised by *Rolling Stone* as the only successful evocation of the sixties milieu, *Another*

Roadside Attraction follows the peregrinations of Amanda, an earth goddess figure; John Paul Ziller, a modern version of the natural man; Plucky Purcell, martial arts expert, benevolent outlaw, and discoverer of the corpse of Jesus Christ in the Roman catacombs; and Marx Marvelous, an East Coast academic studying this group. Michael Rogers attempted to locate the nature of Robbins's successful portrait of the 1960s: "Robbins's success was his realization that the essence of the counterculture was not manners, but fantasy" (Rogers 67). Furthermore, Rogers continues that *Another Roadside Attraction* "was not, in the first place, a realistic novel. It has, in fact, very little to do with reality. And in the end, that is why it will probably remain the most realistic of the counterculture novels."

In 1967 or 1968, Robbins had married for a second time; this wife, Terrie Lunden, and he have a son, Fleetwood Star. The baby was born in 1971, the same year that Ballantine published *Another Roadside Attraction*. Robbins in his youth had fathered another son named Rip, who traveled to Seattle when he was eighteen to meet Robbins and who still resides nearby. (Letter to author 26 June 1995). After three years, Terrie and Tom divorced, but they remain friends. Terrie says that the nearly thirty years that she has known Tom Robbins have been like an extended Jerry Seinfeld show (Interview 1995). They shared custody of Fleetwood, who stayed with his father two or three days of the week. Robbins also supported his son's sports pursuits—soccer, Little League baseball, and out-of-town wrestling matches—when Fleetwood was in his early teens. They live in La Conner. By 1995 Fleetwood had finished college with a degree in popular culture and French; he taught English as a second language for a time. Since, he moved to Prague, currently the site of an expatriate United States youth enclave (Interview 1995).

Robbins's second novel, *Even Cowgirls Get the Blues*, came out in 1976, dedicated to Fleetwood Star. Again reviews were mixed. It was a popular hit regardless of the reviewers. Its publishing history is unusual for the time. For his second book, Robbins enlisted as his agent, Phoebe Larmore, who continues to represent him. Larmore approached the paperback publisher Bantam Books with the manuscript of *Cowgirls* after she learned that Doubleday would pay no more than $7,500 for the rights. Robbins had rejected Doubleday as not sincere in its advertising efforts for *Another Roadside Attraction*. Ted Solotaroff, then senior editor at Bantam, agreed to the $50,000 Larmore requested for volume rights. Because *Another Roadside Attraction* was gaining in popularity at universities, communes, crash pads, and high schools, many publishers were attracted to buying the hardcover rights for *Cowgirls*. When Larmore and Solotaroff auctioned the rights with attached financial requests and a publishing program for future Robbins books, no one made a bid. Buying rights from a paperback company was unprecedented and therefore difficult for hardcover publishers to contemplate. Larmore described the situation as one in which hardcover publishers had "frustration, even an anger, that I'd allow a writer like this to be a paperback author" (Nathan 52). To help arouse interest in the novel, Solotaroff issued a chapter in his journal the *American Review*. *Cowgirls* was excerpted as well in the magazine *High Times* (June 1976).

Larmore then adapted a suggestion from Jack Macrae of Dutton Press and offered publishers the proposal that a small hardback run be published at the same time as a large paperback printing. Robert W. Cowley at Houghton Mifflin in Boston bought the idea and made printing history for its press by publishing the hardback and trade paperback editions simultaneously. A year later, Bantam issued 440,000 copies of its mass market edition. Houghton Mifflin offered 170,000 trade paperbacks in print. Robbins received $50,000 as an advance for *Cowgirls*. By 1980, 1.3 million copies of *Cowgirls* had sold, and in 1995 it went into its forty-third printing. Bantam has remained Robbins's publisher ever since.

In 1977 *Publishers Weekly* was reporting plans for the movie version of *Cowgirls*. Eventually Gus Van Sant directed the film, which was released in 1993. Before this event, Robbins had actually appeared in films. The most famous movie was *Made In Heaven* (1987), directed by Alan Rudolph. He says that he is not pleased with his performance as the toy maker in that film (Edlin 42), but the role is a perfect one for a collecter of rubber stamps and tin toys. His friend Debra Winger persuaded him to appear in the film. He, in turn, wrote an article on Winger for *Esquire* (Feb. 1993); "Confessions of a Reluctant Sex Goddess" portrays Winger as a serious actor whose demand for excellence in her performances wrongly labeled her with the Hollywood epithet "difficult," doom for performers who need job offers. Robbins has also appeared in a docudrama on surrealism by Karl Krogstad and *The Waterman*, independent films. He received his acting card for his voice-over narration of *Cowgirls* (Interview 1994). Before he was a famous director, Van Sant waited in line at a Portland, Oregon, bookstore to meet Robbins, have his copy of *Jitterbug Perfume* autographed, and ask Robbins about the film rights to *Cowgirls* (Horowitz 40). Robbins was accustomed to inquiries about film rights. In fact, he has been quoted as saying that he would believe a film of one of his books is a movie when he has to decide what to wear to the premiere (Strelow 101). The money people in Hollywood sometimes find it difficult to believe a Robbins novel can be filmed. Many directors and actors, however, eagerly pursue rights to his books. Robbins admired Van Sant's previous movies, especially *Drugstore Cowboy* and *My Own Private Idaho*. So when Van Sant indicated that he still wanted to make a film of *Cowgirls*, Robbins was pleased to place it in his hands. Eventually they met in Seattle for dinner. Robbins says that he trusted Van Sant "right away" (Horowitz 40). Unfortunately, critics disliked the film. Robbins refuses to be critical of the movie, even though interviewers try to lead him into negatives. In an unusual perspective, Robbins has suggested that perhaps the film stayed too true to the text of the novel and that his books are difficult to translate to the screen ("Writing"; Interview 1994). Unlike most writers, who complain that screenplay writers and directors don't stay close enough to the original text, Robbins asserts that the screenplay writer should feel free to stray from the written word.

Robbins's most recent movie adventure involves the Algonquin Round Table of Dorothy Parker, Robert Benchley, and other writers, dramatists, and wits of the 1920s and 1930s New York scene. In 1994 Robbins and his fourth wife, Alexa, appeared with speaking parts in Alan Rudolph's film *Mrs. Parker and the Vicious Circle*, in the brothel scene. Alexa greets Robert Benchley as Bobby; Robbins plays a Southern out-of-towner who expresses interest in Mrs. Parker and offers his first-aid expertise after Parker faints. Robbins improvised his dialogue and Rudolph kept much of it in the film. Robbins's great friend Alan Rudolph, to whom, as Maestro Rudolpho, he dedicated *Half Asleep*, and Randy Sue Coburn, another close friend to whom Robbins has read the manuscripts of a couple of his novels in progress, wrote the screenplay for *Mrs. Parker* and have written a screenplay for Robbins's fifth novel, *Skinny Legs and All*. They have strayed from the original text, employing the Painted Stick as narrator for the film. Perhaps Hollywood will recover from the *Cowgirls* box office disappointment and venture a screenplay that contains all the elements to make a film successful. Robbins has no immediate film-acting plans, but Alexa has recently finished appearing in an unreleased independent film.

Robbins is clear about the core value in his novel *Even Cowgirls Get the Blues*. On the set of the movie, Robbins talked with Jonathan Cott about the book: "The goddess is at the core of the book. . . . Sissy, Jellybean, Delores Del Ruby—all are feminine aspects of the Overmind" (62). His main character, Sissy, "represents the end of patriarchy and the reemergence of the female archetype." He adds that Jellybean has to die even though "it upsets me," Robbins says. She must die because "The message that the cowgirls were delivering is that you can fulfill your fantasies. However, that's a very risky proposition, and for me as a writer not to warn the reader of the dangers would have been irresponsible. Because it can be fatal." (Cott 62)

Many women readers responded strongly to *Cowgirls*. Robbins displays a substantial knowledge of feminist issues of the time. One professor has declared *Cowgirls* the first novel in which a female functioned as a hero in the classical sense, as defined by Joseph Campbell in *Hero with a Thousand Faces*. The patriarchal message that natural female body functions need to be masked by feminine deodorizing receives its just debunking when the cowgirls teach the "beauty" ranch clients about female anatomy. Robbins invokes a theory popular at the time connecting female hormonal cycles with the stages of the moon and tides. He also connects with female needs for freedom of movement and sexual expression. He learned much of this material from the women he had known during his life, but his primary informant was his lover at the time of his writing of *Cowgirls*. Libby Burke was a vocalist and strong feminist in the Seattle community. She was outspoken in her beliefs about women's need for freedom. Her bisexuality provided Robbins with a firsthand observation of women making love (Cott 62; Interview 1994). Her feminism exposed Robbins to feminist theories, among them Louise Lacey's theory of the moon's power over the female menstrual cycle (Mitchell 32).

Debate about the feminism, or lack of it, in Robbins's novels nevertheless occurs. Some women find Robbins revolutionary in his treatment of women, praising his respect for females. He may place females on pedestals, but he does not mutilate and chop them into pieces as many contemporary male writers continue to do. Others believe that Robbins exploits his female characters for sexual titillation and caricatures the lesbian cowgirls as extremist, man-hating perversions in *Cowgirls*. People who make this argument point to Bonanza's death at the end of the novel. They see the death as punishment for the cowgirl's lesbian affair, a notion Robbins finds "ridiculously and sadly paranoid" (Interview 1995).

Robbins does believe that feminists have become too extreme in their man hating and sex hating. He admires Camille Paglia, author of *Sexual Personae*, and calls her a maverick feminist because she shakes people out of their complacency and challenges their dogma (Interview 1995). According to Robbins, she also reintroduces sexuality into the discussion of male-female relationships, a focus that Robbins feels is lacking in many feminist discussions. In an article on feminism, Robbins states that some feminists have become their opposite, or macho. He continues with the lament that "It's a rat bite in the heart to observe the deformation of what might have been the most important socio-spiritual awakening in two thousand years" ("Notes on Nukes..." 11). He writes that the money/power syndrome has been responsible for changing feminism into feminismo. Power politics corrupted the movement's spiritual basis. Feminism suffered the same fate as religion, Robbins writes; both became devoid of spirituality in the name of mass-appeal organization (13).

Robbins's books mock all doctrinaire beliefs, whether liberal or conservative. For instance, Robbins places no importance on being "politically correct" as he understands the term. His refusal to conform is Robbins's avenue to growth and creativity. His interpretation of and rejection of the "PC" concept meshes with his treatment of political tyranny in his novels. Art rebels against political control.

Robbins's interest in art of course extends to his own painting. Lacking space, he switched from oil painting to rubber stamp and watercolor collages, completing a series of Buddha collages (McCaffery and Gregory 228). At Richmond his art courses were theory rather than practical courses. The smell of turpentine and the vision of a painting actually emerging on a canvas then captured his imagination and created his desire to write about art, for he did not believe that he could actually paint (McCaffery 228). Recently, however, he returned to painting, executing a series based on the old comic strip character Nancy with the remarkable black hair and bow. Just two titles illustrate the series' concept: "Nancy's Hair Medusa" and "Nancy's Hair Buddha." In both works, Nancy's hair stands alone, removed from the rest of her (Interview 1995).

Of other artists, Robbins is especially fond of the pop masters—Andy Warhol (he owns several Warhol silkscreens) and Claes Oldenburg, the minimal abstractionist—and the color-field painters (McCaffery and Gregory 229). Robbins's art reviews for 1963–1964 were gathered in a xerox copy bound in 1985 by a J. Dille of Seattle and are available in the Seattle Public Library. In 1977 Robbins wrote a tribute to Guy Anderson for the catalogue of Anderson's one-man show at the Seattle Art Museum. Besides being an artist Robbins admires, Anderson is one of Robbins's neighbors (Interview 1995). His paintings are mystical evocations of early myth and natural mysteries of life. Objects meld with the landscape. Oldenburg's stuffed objects inspire Robbins as well. Oldenburg's

art infuses the object with a life of its own. Traditional still lifes by Paul
Cézanne and others also convey that sense of the object as alive to Robbins. The coming to life of a Camel cigarette pack, a spoon, shell, can of
beans, and other objects in Robbins's novels should come as no surprise.

Although no artists are characters in his next work, the artist of the
Camel cigarette package might be pleased by the life his or her sales
packaging achieves in Robbins's imagination. In keeping with his fascination with male/female relationships, "How to Make Love Stay" is the
professed theme of Robbins's book. Robbins's third novel features male
and female protagonists that are opposites attracted to each other. *Still
Life with Woodpecker: A Sort of a Love Story* (1980) was an immediate best-
seller. Bantam paid Robbins a $165,000 advance because of the commer-
cial success of his first two novels. This book, like his others, is still in
print and has been continuously since its first appearance. This "frac-
tured fairytale" (O'Connell 277–79) involves an environmentalist cheerleader of royal blood and an anarchist bomber, the Woodpecker. Both
learn from each other, but the most important lesson is for the princess.
She must recognize that the individual's freedom is more important than
the group. Conformity to a cause and its politics becomes meaningless
and has its own tyranny. By the time *Still Life* appeared, Robbins was
pronounced as "prince of the paperback literati" by Mitchell S. Ross in
the *New York Times Magazine* (1978).

Robbins has continually written articles for magazines and journals,
especially *Esquire*. Besides publishing excerpts from his upcoming novels,
Esquire has used creative articles by Robbins on travel to places such as
the North Canyon in Nevada, covered with Native American petro-
glyphs; Botswana's Okavango delta; and Tanzania. He has also written
articles on Ray Kroc, founder of McDonald's, on soul, and entries for
Esquire's Women We Love and Women of the Year features. One of his
latest feature pieces is on the miniskirt and sixties nostalgia for the *New
York Times*, but his most serious magazine piece is the entry he wrote for
a *Fiction International* special on Writing and Politics. An essay of modest
length, it epitomizes Robbins's values as a writer: an artist concentrates
on language; language is the most important aspect of writing—not plot,
not character—only language.

Jitterbug Perfume (1984), Robbins's fourth novel, was popular like his
other books and spent several months on the *New York Times* best-seller
list. To write this novel he haunted perfume shops and read everything
he could find about perfuming (McCaffery and Gregory 238). The ac-
knowledgments of the book list among others Laren Elizabeth Stover,

who would be the author of the 1995 novel *Pluto, Animal Lover* and who in the early 1980s provided Robbins with perfume industry information, and Jessica Maxwell, "whose ancestor once owned a perfume shop in New Orleans, and who traded me that shop for a flying conch shell." The shop appears in *Jitterbug*. The epilogue called "The Bill" by Robbins is addressed to Darrell Bob Houston, a writer and regular at the Blue Moon. A plaque adorns a booth at the Blue Moon Tavern honoring Darrell Bob Houston. Robbins returned to the Blue Moon for the First Annual Poetry Reading in Memory of Houston.

At about this time Robbins bought a condominium downtown in Seattle and maintained his writing studio/house in La Conner. He had married and divorced a longtime, off-again-on-again love, Donna Davis (Interview 1994; letter to author 15 March 1995). He became romantically involved with an internationally famous glass maker, Ginny Ruffner, and they continue to be close friends (Interview 1994). The eye game that Ellen Cherry Charles plays while riding in the family car in *Skinny Legs* is actually a game Ruffner played as a child (Pall 40). In 1990, when Ruffner was in a serious car accident during a Christmas visit to her parents in Charlotte, North Carolina, Robbins kept a round-the-clock vigil by his friend's side.

Much of his time, though, was devoted to his work. Interviewer Peter Whitmer describes *Jitterbug Perfume* as a celebration of "the joy of individual expression and self-reliance" (52). He distinguishes Robbins from other socially conscious writers because Robbins "brings us alternatives and solutions; constructive plans that build on optimism" (52). Joy is crucial to Robbins, but, as he has said, "joy in spite of everything." He dislikes a lot of current literature because it indulges in hand-wringing and whining—"dreary little dramas of domestic discord"—and because it traffics in misery and violence. In a 1985 interview Robbins declared that he doesn't hang out with other writers because he believes that many writers suffer from alcoholism and are often depressed, glum, and self-pitying as a result of the disease.

> Therefore, what we have in America right now is a diseased literature. Most novelists write about twisted, unhappy lives. As a character in *Jitterbug Perfume* says, "Unhappiness is the ultimate self-indulgence." You should deal with your problems and turn them from lead into gold. Many novels are only turning lead into denser lead. (Dougherty 124)

Despite his rejection of the angry alcoholics, Robbins does respect many writers. The list varies according to the stage or time in his life. James Joyce, Blaise Cendrars, Henry Miller, Lewis Carroll, Herman Hesse, Ishmael Reed, Thomas Pynchon, Nancy Lemann, Isabel Allende, and Gabriel Garcia Marquez are among the authors he often cites ("Writing": Interview 1995; letter enclosure 15 March 1995). Most of the authors he admires experiment and play with language or explore certain aspects of spirituality. Although not fond of social realist writers, he praises Jim Harrison's style and respects William Faulkner.

In another interview Robbins has declared that being famous or having a reputation as a great writer were not his interests, although the money is always nice (1995). Rigid authorial egos create unhappiness in Robbins's opinion, but individual creativity and self-expression are necessary for the creation of great art. The artist needs to be able to see beyond the limits mass society imposes with its standardization, advertising, and media. Governments are afraid of creativity and mind expansion because these qualities threaten the status quo of government control. Robbins reiterates these ideas throughout his novels. He also stresses that too many contemporary novelists feel sorry for themselves, exploit and revel in their violent behavior, and dwell on victimization. These "realist" writers fail to offer any positive alternatives to the wretched world they observe.

Robbins moves beyond the complaints and criticisms that are so easy to make and sees the humor and potential for good in life and in people. In *Jitterbug Perfume* three parfumiers search for the final ingredient to the perfect perfume. Each searches because of greed or artistic desire. Robbins has the artistic conquer greed in a conclusion that uses the female principle of cooperation among the three artists. They all plan to share in dividing up the "profits" of the perfume. Immortals interfere in their plans; nature foils again the human quest for immortality and lasting love.

In Robbins's fifth novel art and greed, among other institutions, struggle against each other. *Skinny Legs and All* (1990) is known as Robbins's most political novel. Part of the book focuses on an Arab and a Jew who open a restaurant together across the street from the U.N. Building in New York City. Political groups that want to keep the Arab-Israeli conflict active keep bombing their business. This novel includes animate inanimate objects as characters who are seeking reunion with the Levantine goddess, Astarte. Robbins's visit to Israel provided much background for *Skinny Legs and All*. His study of the mother goddess and patriarchy's banishment of goddess worship is one of the major themes of the novel. Again he suggests that a return to the feminine principle would lessen the violence and injustice that are ruining the world. Robbins by no means favors goddess worship, however, since he strongly believes that the divine is neither masculine nor feminine (Interview 1995).

An excerpt of *Skinny Legs* appeared in *Esquire* magazine in April of 1990. (Bantam at that time reissued all of Robbins's novels with new covers designed by him, though he did not do the final artwork.) Reviews of the new novel were again mixed. Most reviewers admire Robbins's language. Many reviewers complain that his serious presentation of troublesome issues such as religious fundamentalism and religious hate, male and female relationships, the shallow art world and pretend artists, and sexuality fail in this novel. They prefer Robbins's humor. Other reviewers criticize Robbins's humor, too. Robbins began ignoring critics earlier in his career. *Still Life with Woodpecker* is his response to reviewers, one writer has declared (Mitchell 32). When asked about his rejection by some establishment book reviewers and academics, Robbins compares them to mice running around in the attic; one hears the scamper of their little feet and occasionally comes across their droppings, but they're very easy to ignore (Interview 1994; "Writing from the Inside Out"). Robbins enjoyed his book tour of Great Britain because "the critics had actually read the novel" (Interview March 1995). Ultimately, though, it is the reader who is important to him. He is delighted that younger people enjoy his books because they are the generation that will influence society's future.

Hundreds of people, not all young by any means, did wait in line on a warm, muggy Seattle night in August of 1994 when *Half Asleep in Frog Pajamas* came out. Robbins signed for five hours that night. And the signing at Elliott Bay Bookstore was the first on a list of publicity interviews and appearances. *Half Asleep* focuses on the dark nineties when greed and exploitation, violence, and homelessness seem unsolvable social realities. Added to those societal woes is the destruction of the planet as an ecosystem that will finally not be able to support human life because of its deterioration. Robbins traveled to Timbuktu to see the legendary city that everyone threatens people with as the most dreaded of destinations (Interview 1994). He also went to investigate the beliefs that two separate African peoples, the Bozo and the Dogon, hold in their folklore that amphibious beings from outer space came down to earth thousands of years ago. At the end of the novel, Robbins provides a bibliography of sources that interested readers may consult about these peoples and their beliefs. Robbins gathered information firsthand about the Bozo and the Dogon and their environment when he visited.

Half Asleep in Frog Pajamas spent a few weeks on the *New York Times* best-seller list and sold well. Bantam published the volume in hardback for the first edition, then a trade paperback version. As a promotion for the book, Bantam distributed nightcaps with the traditional long, floppy, pointed top to select bookstores for their sales force. During an interview on National Public Radio, Robbins described the protagonist's discovery of the Bozo and Dogons' beliefs as a rending of the "fabric of consensual reality" (Hansen 39). The novel, therefore, casts doubt on traditional Western versions of reality.

As usual, Robbins traveled the United States and England to promote the book. He appeared on talk shows and radio interview programs such as National Public Radio's *Weekend Edition*. One student organization at Yale University featured Robbins as Hensen Professor for the Day. Besides meeting with the students, he also gave a public lecture. The Yale University Department of English did not sponsor the lecture, perhaps illustrating the snubbing that academics usually give Robbins. He is not "serious" enough for the academy or academic presses. Two people have written dissertations on or including Robbins. Marc Siegel of the University of Wyoming has written the longest published work on Robbins, a 1980 monograph of fifty-two pages, published in the Boise State University Western Writers Series.

Robbins believes that a work of art should be considered without the author's biography or assumed intention. He states that parts of him are in each of his characters, just as parts of people that he knows or has observed are in his characters (Interview 1995). Events in his novels are actually closer to truth than people want to believe. Furthermore, he agrees with those who claim that the author no longer owns the text after it is published. His views coincide with the academic theories of the postmodern era. As an illustration of his attitude, Robbins, when requested to do so, nonchalantly signed copies of a derivative book a public relations man had written and self-published. He is now being sued by the author, who claimed that Robbins was representing himself as the book's author.

Robbins's house in La Conner is the last house on a dead-end road on the Swinomish Indian Reservation. His two-bedroom 1970s bungalow has a multitude of large windows opening onto scenes of the Puget Sound. The limited remodeling that he and his wife have done includes frog tiles as a backsplash, a motif repeated in his studio/house in La Conner village. Their yard extends down to the water. If they walk down the hill to the beach, they can watch seals, dolphins, and an occasional whale. It's a perfect place to do meditation and yoga, which Robbins does every day with the Salute to the Sun (Interview 1995). Robbins sold his condominium in Seattle to settle more in La Conner.

Robbins recently purchased a computer but has no intention of writing on it. All of his novels have been written in longhand (sometimes long passages of dialogue may be typed on an old Remington) at an old roll-topped desk in his studio writing room surrounded by views of the trees in his yard. He begins his novels with only the structure in mind. He does not outline or overly plan a plot (Hensen 38). *Cowgirls* and *Skinny Legs* started with only their titles (Egan "Perfect" C9). Sometimes characters introduce themselves to him as if auditioning. Some he admits to the story. After resisting the inanimates in *Skinny Legs*, he finally allowed them to join the narrative. He had not originally planned on Shell, Painted Stick, Can o' Beans, Sock, or Spoon as part of the novel. He deliberately allows the "situation" and the language to come to him as he sits in his writing studio (Hansen 40–41). Adventure is his experience when writing a book; adventure is the reader's as well.

Robbins continues to learn the mysteries of the computer and increase his knowledge of French. His encyclopedic mind will perhaps create a mélange of the two for his seventh novel. In the meantime, his six novels provide enough information, entertainment, and provocation to keep readers arguing over Robbins's merits.

2

Context and Style

Tom Robbins's novels regularly reach the best-seller list. Because of their popularity, Robbins's novels are suspect to self-proclaimed experts such as critics and scholars. If a writer is popular, the logic goes, she or he must be writing superficial pap. The writing cannot be of a high quality, the view further goes, if the mass of readers like it. Such writers forget that the public has taste and a desire to be entertained. Tom Robbins's novels appeal to the public's taste for entertainment and humor. Robbins envelops his social commentary in humor and rich language. His philosophies and his playfulness with language appeal to the imagination. His books stretch the right brain by the creative use of language and image that he employs; furthermore, Robbins's fantasies challenge the imagination to a willing suspension of disbelief beyond the usual demands made by fiction. Robbins also suggests life-affirming alternatives to the depressing negatives of the most valued novel writing. His novels offer profound insights into the mess of the world that the majority of writers portray. Robbins writes of individuality and individual responsibility for a person's life and actions; the individual's behavior affects the rest of the world, including the natural environment. Combining his knowledge of Eastern philosophies and quantum physics, Robbins articulates the maxim that everything is connected. He uses an example from chaos theory in *Another Roadside Attraction* which explains this concept. If a butterfly flutters its wings in Brazil, for instance, the motion will influence the weather for the rest of the world. No action, animal, or person exists in isolation from the world. Robert Nadeau writes of Robbins's use of quantum physics and philosophy. In his novels, Nadeau asserts, Robbins employs these constructs not to suggest that Westerners adopt the Eastern philosophical perspective but rather "to hammer away relentlessly at those assumptions about self and world in western cosmology which he feels are injurious to our safety as well as our emotional and psychological well-being" (65). Robbins's novels question the basis of Western philosophy.

Robbins's leaps of imagination and language challenge the literal minded and conservative. Placing him in the context of literary history is not an easy task because he amalgamates techniques from several eras of novel writing, crystalizing them into a mélange of his own which has no accurate imitators, although several wanna-bes. His "episodic style" of writing originates from Robbins's reading of John Cage's *Silence*, which uses the Zen Koan form (McCaffery & Gregory 226). Robbins sprinkles allusions to other philosophers and writers throughout his novels, so it is appropriate to place him within the context of literary history. He swears that he has never studied eighteenth-century English novels, but the epistolary style—the telling of a narrative through letters—dominates *Another Roadside Attraction*, his first novel, and letters figure prominently in his subsequent novels as well. In the eighteenth century, Daniel DeFoe adopted this narrative form in his novels based on fictitious lives of renegades. DeFoe justified his tales of love and adventure by claiming moral lessons as their purpose. Samuel Richardson began publishing novels about the lives of young women, using letters between the heroines and their friends and family members as the method of telling the narrative. Richardson's novel *Pamela* (1740–41) related the story of a servant girl who withheld her sexual favors from an impertinent and importunate employer. Her virtue is rewarded because her employer eventually marries her. Other stories told by letters include the novel *Clarissa Harlowe* (1747–48), which features the letters of a young woman who is kidnapped, imprisoned, and raped by a man who attracts her. These novels began a tradition of letter use as a means of developing the events of a narrative. Robbins continues this method of development by including letters and adding diary entries in his narratives.

Robbins has another precedent in the eighteenth century; his fantasy and word play, exemplified in his practice of including nonsense syllables and neologisms, or invented words, parallels *The Life and Opinions of Tristram Shandy* (1759–67) by the experimental novelist Laurence Sterne LeClain. In *Tristram Shandy*, the developing fetus of Tristram narrates events before and up to his birth, ending the story with his delivery. The language play and fantasy of Sterne, an eighteenth-century novelist famous for his experiments with the narrative form, are echoed in Robbins's style. Robbins, however, says that he has never read Sterne (Interview 1994). Robbins has therefore chanced upon a style in his novels that has roots in the eighteenth century. Since one of his themes is that everything is connected, it makes perfect sense that his style harkens back to a centuries-old technique. When critics dismiss his work as frivolous, they contradict the praise of academics for the highly regarded origins of the novel in English.

But Robbins does not simply reproduce, even accidentally, the style of the early English novel. He advances the narrative by mixing the letter writing of the epistolary novel into a third-person narrative report and adds a series of diary entries to provide information missing from the narrator's range of knowledge. Furthermore, Robbins writes synchronically rather than chronologically. In other words, he attempts to convey events that are happening simultaneously around the world or across town by switching his narrator from one consciousness to another. This movement from one mind to another had its advent in the development of psychological theories of the mind as multileveled with a conscious and an unconscious. Sigmund Freud, the Viennese physician and developer of psychoanalysis, studied the latest theories of the human mind that physicians in France had discovered. He continued research into understanding illness such as hysteria, often a paralysis thought to be caused by the mind, and developed several theories of the psychology of the human mind, including the multilevel consciousness which the twentieth century has universally embraced. Freudian psychological theory influenced many British writers during the early twentieth century. These writers experimented with the point of view employed in their novels; they also sought new ways to express the multilevel workings of the mind. The style of syntax these writers adopted attempts to recreate the abrupt shifts in ideas, images, and senses that occur as the mind free-associates and interprets the emotional, factual, and sensual information that it absorbs. The critic and novelist May Sinclair borrowed the term "stream of consciousness," from the psychological theories of the American philosopher William James, to describe this experimental kind of writing. James Joyce, Dorothy Richardson, May Sinclair, and Virginia Woolf are examples of English stream of consciousness writers. The French novelist Marcel Proust receives credit as the originator in any language of this writing style. Robbins extends the manipulation of language and sounds that these writers initiated.

Besides the changes from topic to topic or impression to impression of the stream of consciousness style, these writers used nonsense syllables, incomplete sentences, and neologisms to express the internal workings of the mind. Tom Robbins has adopted this aspect of the psychological writers. He does not attempt to develop the deep psychological levels of his characters' minds, but he does appropriate the playful nature of language. Among the writers that he cites regularly as his influences, Robbins includes James Joyce, who is the primary twentieth-century language inventor and experimentalist (Strelow 101; Enclosure letter to author, 15 March 1995). Joyce's last novel, *Finnegans Wake* (1939), challenges readers with its continuous play of nonsense syllables, neologisms, and apparent non sequiturs. It is often cited as unreadable or at the least very difficult to read. Although he never sacrifices readability, Robbins admires Joyce's concentration on language. Furthermore, Robbins has declared that language is his primary ("Writing and Politics") preoccupation rather than character or plot development ("Writing and Politics").

Besides the language play and fantasy that characterize Robbins's writing, point of view experiments constitute another identifiable trait of Robbins's narrative style. Robbins shares the stream of consciousness writers' fascination with point of view, but he does not attempt to use it as a method of insight into or recreation of the workings of the human mind and emotion. Robbins disclaims any attempts to call him a realist; he is not attempting to be realistic like the psychological novelists of the early twentieth century. On the contrary, he classifies himself as a romantic writer and repeatedly calls attention to the artificiality of the writing act (Interview 1994; McCaffery & Gregory 226; O'Connell 273). In his first two novels, *Another Roadside Attraction* and *Even Cowgirls Get the Blues*, characters tell the story in third person even though they are personally involved with parts of the narrative. These narrators, Marx Marvelous and Dr. Robbins, withhold their identity until late in the novel, pretending to be disinterested parties even though both are attracted to the female protagonists whose lives they are recording. Marx Marvelous reveals his love for Amanda before his identity as narrator, but he uses a third-person observer point of view and claims to be a reporter of events. Throughout Robbins's novels, narrative voices interrupt the text with comments about the process of writing, accentuating the artificiality of the narrative process. He describes these interruptions as an "attempt to make the novel less abstract, more of a real thing" (McCaffery & Gregory 229). Always pursuing new methods of expressing the narrative, Robbins continues to experiment with point of view. He reminds readers that a text is a created construct.

In his latest novel, *Half Asleep in Frog Pajamas*, Robbins uses second person as the narrative point of view. Employing "you" throughout a novel as the voice of the narrator is highly unconventional. The narrator addresses the reader as though the reader were the main character, Gwen Mati. This deliberate connection of the main character's values and traits to the reader and also to the protagonist creates a tension between the reader and the text. If the reader will not or cannot identify with the character, the novel will not be successful. Additionally, since the character is not wholly admirable, Robbins risks a total rejection from the reader because the reader refuses to suspend his or her disbelief. This use of "you" also reads as though a disembodied voice is telling the protagonist her life. It is perhaps a tarot card reader telling a client her past, hinting about the future. Or it is a voice inside the head of the protagonist telling her what she is doing and feeling. Since Gwen's neighbor and friend is the tarot reader Q-Jo Huffington who disappears, it is entirely possible that Robbins intends that the second person sound like a tarot reader. This second-person point of view is so revolutionary that the Quality Paperback Book Club advertises the novel as "Told Entirely in the Second Person."

Just as scholars study the original English novels to gain insight into the cultural and social concerns of its writers and their times, scholars will study Robbins's novels as clues to social and cultural issues of the later half of the twentieth century in the United States. In the context of United States writing, Robbins continues the American tradition of heroes who head out for the territories, as Huck Finn first said. Although Robbins derives the road novel from a long history of literary texts, he revises the tradition by using females as the focal point of his road adventures. In *Even Cowgirls Get the Blues*, he pays homage to the ultimate American road novelist from the previous generation of writers, Jack Kerouac, pretending that Sissy Hankshaw, his female hitchhiker hero, spent some time as a friend of Kerouac.

Robbins has been described as "one of the daddies of pop culture" (Karbo) and as a cult figure (Batchelor 19). He gained the attention of college students when *Another Roadside Attraction* came out in paperback and made him an underground cult writer for the university crowd. *Even Cow-*

girls Get the Blues sealed his position as cult hero and writer of the counter-cultural. College students, former children of the sixties, and women rallied to Robbins and his challenges to patriarchal institutions, especially organized religion. Robbins's novels continue to reach the best-seller lists. Although he feels that he has lost the attention of those in their twenties, he maintains popularity with his earliest followers, baby boomers, and sixteen- to eighteen-year-olds. He says that he lost those in between these ages because "I am no longer considered subversive" (Edlin 42).

Robbins has variously been grouped in reviews and articles with avant-garde writers Thomas Pynchon, Kurt Vonnegut, John Irving, Richard Brautigan, and Robert Pirsig. The connection between Robbins and Pynchon is the strongest. Both writers play with language, use many puns, have strong female characters as protagonists for their novels (Pynchon's *The Crying of Lot 49* features Oedipa Maas), provide dense amounts of factual information, and use fantasy. They share a kindred stylistic spirit but interpret the world from different perspectives. Their affinity is great enough, however, that a letter from Pynchon forms a publicity blurb on the frontispiece of *Even Cowgirls Get the Blues*.

Whereas Pynchon comes closest to a kindred spirit to Robbins, other writers share the concerns of Robbins. One reviewer of *Jitterbug Perfume* declared Robbins the "Vonnegut of the Eighties: the age of the Yuppie, Semper Perrier and all that quiche" (KJG, *West Coast Review of Books*). In keeping with the 1980s pursuit of money, the characters of *Jitterbug Perfume* compete with one another to discover the key ingredient to a superperfume which arouses passion. The competition is based on a combination of greed and devotion to the craft of parfumier. Robbins punctures the 1980s ethos by undermining the characters' competitiveness. Eventually, in an anticapitalistic ending, the group of competitors unite in a win-win situation, as business jargon has it, and work together on the production of the perfume. These characters represent the entrepreneurial drive of the eighties. Tempered by the love of their craft, they defeat their individual greed in favor of a collective production of their art. Robbins's novel offers a corrective to the ruthless enterprise of business—a world in which art wins.

Shifra Sharlin wrote a review essay for *Books & Religion* in 1990, coining "theography" as a term for a new novel genre which she sees as having emerged in the 1970s. In this review, Sharlin classes together Robbins's *Another Roadside Attraction*, Kurt Vonnegut's *Cat's Cradle*, Robert Pirsig's *Zen and the Art of Motorcycle Maintenance*, and Richard Bach's *Jonathan Livingston Seagull* as polymorphic theographic novels. She regards these novels as typical of the 1970s efforts to deal with spirituality and religion. Their efforts result in books about the nuclear age that find multiple godheads appealing rather than one god. In the 1990s Sharlin sees the theographic novelists as "monogamous monotheists." These novelists, represented by Salman Rushdie's *The Satanic Verses*, N. Scott Momaday's *The Ancient Child*, John Irving's *Prayer for Owen Meany*, James Morrow's *Only Begotten Daughter*, and Michael Downing's *Mother of God*, cling to "their traditional religion in a threatening secular world" (5). Sharlin describes Robbins and Vonnegut as "trying to escape via their high priestesses, high jinx, and highs" the evils of the world which Robert Pirsig spends "laboriously" analyzing. The synergy between the novelists of the 1970s polymorphs is such that Robbins unknowingly quoted from his fellow polytheist Vonnegut's *Cat's Cradle*: "Certain travel suggestions are dancing lessons from God" in *Another Roadside Attraction* (Sharlin 6; McCaffery & Gregory 235).[1] The free-spirited promiscuous polymorphs find alternatives to the death-worshipping world by pursuing nature, sex, the "random, the arbitrary, and the whimsical" (Sharlin 5). Sharlin's analysis of these novels of the 1970s clarifies the context for their tone and enlightens readers with insights into the serious issues these whimsical novels actually are exploring. Robbins chafes against the belief that humor and whimsy exclude the serious.

Robbins's positive challenges to the mainstream differ radically from the texts of writers who are regarded as more serious American authors. Saul Bellow and John Cheever, for instance, are writers of an upper middle-class world stuck in traditional values and bored to death and depression. None of the characters move beyond these worlds; they try mindless methods of coping, only to find themselves more depressed and confused. The world is a terrible place, they conclude, and proceed to drink or fornicate themselves into momentary oblivion. According to Robbins, "Comic writing is not only more profound than tragedy, it's a hell of a lot more difficult to write" (McCaffery and Gregory 236). Exploring pain is more important to the critics than exploring joy, Robbins complains, adding that this attitude seems insane. Robbins's characters search for creativity and positively engage with the world. They do not allow depression to overwhelm them; in *Jitterbug Perfume* Robbins has Wiggs Dannyboy declare unhappiness as the "ultimate form o'self indulgence" (210). Robbins moves beyond the doom-and-gloom writing of many high art authors to explore constructive and positive fantasies. His characters' quests for self-fulfillment are positive rather than self-destructive.

CHARACTERS

In the spirit of the novels of the sixties and seventies, popular writers examined alternative lifestyles or challenged the status quo of society. The protests against the war in Vietnam and the near impeachment of the president of the United States, Richard Nixon, are two examples of nationwide and global events that placed in question the validity of the government and the belief in the reliability of the government. Many people rejected the traditional values of the United States when such corruption became widely known. Disillusion dominated much of the discourse of this time, and many novelists explored these new visions of the world. Robbins did not give in to doubt and self-pity; he had already realized that vast organizations such as governments and religions operated for the benefit of the hierarchy rather than the common good. His texts moved beyond disillusion to explore the power of individuals to create positive versions of the world. The characters in Robbins's novels are usually on the fringe of society in their gender, origins, lifestyle, or their point of view. They are liberated from the status quo, and this freedom allows them to pursue their true selves and creativity, establishing a positive environment of respect for others and for nature. Those characters who conform to a traditional perspective or profile become challenged during the narrative and evolve into a higher spiritual or creative energy or lose their comfortable self-satisfaction. Gwen Mati in *Half Asleep in Frog Pajamas* begins the novel as a happy, self-satisfied stockbroker who has just learned that her easy money and life of materialism have been shattered by a stock market crash. As a Filipina and a female, Gwen is a double outsider to the Wall Street world, but she has entered the mainstream by amassing success financially. Similarly, Marx Marvelous in *Another Roadside Attraction* seeks out Amanda at the roadside zoo as a research subject because he is a scientist trained in the traditional rational logic of the West. His world is challenged by Amanda's perspective, and Marx learns to appreciate the intuitive and natural.

Both Gwen and Marx reach different levels of consciousness from their original complacencies in the mainstream, but Julian Gitche in *Even Cowgirls Get the Blues* remains inside the mainstream that he has struggled so hard to enter. He rejects his Mohawk origins in favor of the Ivy League education his parents provided him. His parents became rich as entrepreneurs and reject their Native American origins as well; Julian has successfully fulfilled their dreams of acceptance in the white world.

When Julian cannot recognize the wisdom of his wife's self-acceptance but rather regards her as insane, he must lose Sissy. These characters are a few examples of those who either meet the challenge to their complacency or lose the opportunity for evolution.

In addition to those characters who greet the challenges to the status quo with openness or rejection, Robbins populates his novels with characters that fulfill or overthrow ever-present archetypes. Robbins's use of archetypes is a natural extension of his study of philosophy and myth, particularly the work of Joseph Campbell, Robert Graves, and Buddhist scholars. Robbins distinguishes his texts with the female heroes that he creates. They are independent and strong women who are open to the universe and nature. Many of the women in Robbins's novels represent goddesses. The women are superior to the men in their understanding of the connections among all objects and living beings on the planet. Amanda in *Another Roadside Attraction* and Sissy in *Even Cowgirls Get the Blues* epitomize the earth goddess. They are fertile mothers who initiate men into an understanding of the interconnectedness of life. Amanda performs this task for Marx Marvelous and Sissy, for Dr. Robbins. Amanda appears born with this understanding of and appreciation of nature. As a young girl, she studied butterflies and learned about edible plants. She wanders in the forest, surviving on the edibles, especially mushrooms. In *Cowgirls* Sissy learns to appreciate her instincts and innate knowledge of the universe after her marriage to Julian Gitche distracts her from her natural self and causes her to doubt the validity of her love of freedom and self-expression. Sissy regains her self-confidence after her renewal with the cowgirls at the Rubber Rose Ranch and her final induction into an understanding of herself and the Clock People by the Chink. Now an earth mother, Sissy becomes pregnant from her encounters with the Chink, the wise Japanese-American. The Chink pronounces her the mother of a future generation of peaceful people, unable to use lethal weapons because of their oversized thumbs. Ellen Cherry Charles in *Skinny Legs and All* sees the Phoenician Queen Jezebel as her "eternal double" (25). Queen Jezebel worshipped the goddess Astarte and was condemned for the practice by jealous male officialdom, who found the cult of Astarte a threat to their religious monopoly. As a challenger to patriarchy, Ellen Cherry Charles defies her fundamentalist Baptist preacher uncle and her father by studying art, going to college, living in New York, and wearing the makeup and stiletto heels they deem worthy only of a Jezebel. Princess Leigh-Cheri in *Still Life with Woodpecker: A Sort of a Love Story* represents the fairy-tale princess as absurdity.

She devotes herself to environmental causes until she meets an anarchist bomber, Bernard Mickey Wrangle, known as the Woodpecker, and falls in love. In a misplaced romantic notion of true love, she incarcerates herself in the family attic and lives in a self-created jail while her Woodpecker serves prison time for his past bombing efforts. Robbins reverses the fairy-tale purity of the princess, her helplessness, and the reward of true love from a dashing prince in this novel. Beginning the novel as the opposite of a prince, Bernard does not save ideals for people, he destroys them. Ultimately the Woodpecker becomes her prince; Princess Leigh-Cheri rescues Bernard after they have been buried in a pyramid her affianced Arab sheik has been building to earn her love. Despite Robbins's reversal of the fairy-tale princess as pure—Leigh-Cheri is a pregnant teenaged cheerleader—Leigh-Cheri does end her life with her true love, Bernard. After the rescue, she and Woodpecker live together in domestic bliss, unable to hear each other because they lost their hearing in the blast that destroys the pyramid. The romantic Robbins closes the novel with a bittersweet relationship based on a lack of communication both before and after the hearing loss. Leigh-Cheri serves as the goddess of love or the moon gone awry. The novel is divided into the phases of the moon. The moon goddess is another form of the great mother goddess, Robbins informs readers, and *Still Life* continues the goddess symbolism Robbins has used in his two previous novels (189).[2]

Kudra in *Jitterbug Perfume* serves as another eternal mother goddess. After centuries of initiating Alobar into the equality and spirit of love, Kudra transcends life literally, leaving Alobar behind on earth. Alobar is supposed to transcend with her, but is unable to let go of the earth. Alobar wants to bring back Kudra to earth and life. He also will continue his immortality if he can reunite with her. The mother goddess myth focuses on a continual rejuvenation and eternality. Alobar cannot transcend his life on earth and seeks to continue his earthly immortality through his love of Kudra, mother goddess. Even the most perfect love cannot last, Robbins shows, but a celebration of love and life through collaboration and creativity instead of competition can salvage humanity and provide happiness.

In *Half Asleep in Frog Pajamas* Q-Jo Huffington, tarot card reader, obese, and friend of the protagonist, Gwen Mati, disappears much as Kudra in *Jitterbug Perfume* transcends life. Q-Jo is in the airwaves just as Kudra is, Robbins hints, as she appears a ghostly figure on the television in Larry's apartment. Gwen spends the novel running around Seattle in search of her boyfriend's orangutan, of Larry Diamond, her only hope of saving her career because of his stock market abilities, and of her lost sense of self because the stock market crash has destroyed her self-complacency and her career. Q-Jo represents an underlying preoccupation of Gwen's because Larry hints that Q-Jo has achieved the ability to transcend life. Gwen wonders and worries about her friend's safety, whereas Robbins portrays her as above the scramble for livelihood and life which Gwen and Larry frantically embrace. Q-Jo connects with the frog spirits that have disappeared from the planet earth. Q-Jo is the earth goddess who abandons an earth embroiled in fruitless materialism and destruction of the planet. Larry regards Gwen as the earth goddess repressed and self-alienated. Gwen simply needs to get in touch with her primal sexual self, which lies buried under the white patriarchal values that she has pursued in an attempt to negate her basic Filipina values. Furthermore, she rejects the emotional and creative legacies from her mother, a poet, who commits suicide by sticking her head in an oven, and her father, a jazz musician who lives a marginal lifestyle. In sketching Gwen's mother, Robbins alludes to the suicide of American poet Sylvia Plath. Gwen's denial of her parents effectively stifles the spontaneous emotional, sexual, and creative sides of herself.

THEMES

Before Robbins was called the Vonnegut of the eighties, he was a cult writer of the seventies. Robbins actually has aged his novels incrementally by setting them in successive half decades. His novels reflect contemporary preoccupations with life and death. These reflections shift according to the emphasis of the current decade or half of it. Robbins's *Skinny Legs and All* is divided into seven sections, paralleling the fabled Dance of the Seven Veils. The symbolism Robbins assigns to each veil represents an issue that regularly occurs in his novels and is featured in each section of the novel. These veils serve as humanity's methods of coping with life and its dilemmas. His first novel, *Another Roadside Attraction*, established his ability to capture the atmosphere of the sixties; in fact, the novel has been declared the one successful recreation of the sixties ambiance. Instead of writing about acid trips or communal living, Robbins uses point of view and narrative structure to create the atmosphere. He deliberately set out to construct the narrative in concentric circles, working on this structure for two years (Interview, August 1994). The role of religion and the nature of spirituality dominate this book.

According to Marx Marvelous, organized religion serves as one of the veils people use to live their lives (159–165). People hide behind organized religion instead of deciding for themselves a moral code and philosophy of life.

Embracing life rather than pursuing death is a major Robbins theme, and *Jitterbug Perfume* focuses primarily on it. Alobar is a thousand-year-old man who opens the narrative as the fertility king of an ancient society; he continues in immortality through the help of a wise shaman, monks, and mysterious cave dwellers, the Bandaloops. In addition to immortality, Alobar and his immortal love, Kudra, attempt to find a perfume that will camouflage the smell of the god Pan and serve as their signature scent to tell each other where they are; Alobar discovers the needed base note to the perfume as he is transcending, returns to earth and creates the perfect scent, K23. Kudra continues to transcend life, but Alobar cannot relinquish life in this world. He spends many centuries attempting to reunite with Kudra. Robbins continues in this novel a theme begun in *Still Life with Woodpecker*. In that novel Robbins poses the conundrum and quest for its characters as "how to make love stay" (4). In *Jitterbug Perfume* Robbins continues his concern about love but dominates it by the search for immortality. Defeating death becomes Alobar's quest, and later, in *Half Asleep in Frog Pajamas*, Larry Diamond chases after a cure for the rectal cancer he suffers, just as other Robbins characters hope to defeat death. Robbins emphasizes that life in the present condition is all that people know for certain and, therefore, life should be joyful.

In keeping with the ideology of the 1960s, Robbins routinely criticizes institutions. Organized religion, the Roman Catholic Church especially, receives Robbins's censure. He criticizes organized religions that promise a better life after death and that valorize suffering in this life on earth. *Another Roadside Attraction* speculates on the premise that Jesus' body did not transcend, as biblical texts claim, but actually remains buried underneath the Vatican. The entire Roman Catholic Church as well as Christianity are based on a hoax. Roman Catholic beliefs are established on fraudulent claims by an inner circle who continue to exploit, murder, and rob people in the name of this lie.

In addition to Roman Catholicism, Robbins criticizes fundamentalist Baptists and radical Jews and Arabs in *Skinny Legs and All*. In this novel, Robbins creates the most overt political statement of his oeuvre. Organized religions become superseded by fanatics who believe murder is the only solution to their desire to control the world. The history of this fanaticism dates back to the earliest religions when goddess worship, particularly of Astarte, was outlawed. A return to goddess worship becomes the solution to world religious strife and hate in *Skinny Legs*. Those people who are not religious fanatics have become football fanatics. Robbins has his characters Spike and Abu schedule the performance of the sacred Dance of the Seven Veils on the same night as the Super Bowl, which Robbins depicts as the American replacement for religion. The Dance of the Seven Veils lures men away from the Super Bowl and reasserts the deep psychological and instinctual appeal of the feminine spirit. A return to the female will salve the wounds to the world that male dichotomous thinking has caused.

As in *Skinny Legs*, in other Robbins novels a return to the female principle also provides an answer to world chaos and pain. Debbie in *Even Cowgirls Get the Blues* declares that women must educate men about the feminine circle to deflect men from the dualism, square shapes, and Cartesian philosophy that have lulled people into perceiving them as logical and, therefore, as the only way to look at the world. The feminine circle, which shows that all life is connected, will save the planet from the destructive and exploitive worldview of the patriarchy.

A return to the female circle in *Cowgirls* carries further *Another Roadside Attraction*'s initial presentation of the female as the spiritual answer to the social and political woes of the modern United States. Amanda, the protagonist of *Roadside*, is the emotional and spiritual antidote to the corruption of the Roman Catholic Church and the deterioration of religious and spiritual health in the United States. The scientist Marx Marvelous chooses to study Amanda and her friends to understand as a spiritual approach that which disenchanted Americans are pursuing in attempts to fill the void that intolerant organized religion has left in their lives. As a way to connect with an understanding of the female spirit, Amanda in *Roadside* and Delores del Ruby in *Cowgirls* ingest the circular peyote button hallucinogen. Robbins implies that by losing logical inhibitions through certain drugs humans reconnect with the female principle of intuition, peaceful means, harmony with nature, and spirituality. Sex and creative expression also can provide the reconnection with the goddess principle that Robbins suggests as the means of saving the human race from a self-destructive doom.

His second novel, *Even Cowgirls Get the Blues*, captures the tensions of the women's movement of the early seventies. Self-fulfillment and the interconnection of all life forms serve as two central foci of the book. Bonanza Jellybean is caught between the radical politics of Delores Del

Ruby and her own milder goals for women to be free to pursue the profession of cowpoke if she so desires. Sissy Hankshaw struggles between her need for the self-expression of her natural talents and her desire to conform to the norms of wifehood and retain her husband. Amongst this turmoil Robbins celebrates female sexual expression. In this description of women loving women and women enjoying sex, Robbins parallels another writer of the 1970s, Erica Jong, whose *Fear of Flying* is the first frank and open portrait of female sexual desire and fantasy in American literature. In Robbins, women's body parts are not employed as invective or unseemly language; rather they are named as neutral or desirable parts of a female anatomy without the degrading connotations associated with sexist slang for the female body. Robbins shares the trend in expanding slang vocabulary into everyday conversation that characterized the sixties and seventies, but he does not incorporate cursing. Few of his characters actually swear, and those that do are suspect in their political outlook. Robbins portrays an open sexuality that is positive and life affirming in his novels, but *Cowgirls* dwells particularly on the issue of female sexual desire. Furthermore, Robbins exposes the deadliness of the oppression of others, especially by sexism, in *Cowgirls*. This oppression serves as another veil that keeps humans from taking responsibility for their own lives.

A rejection of organized religion and a return to the worship and appreciation of the female principles of sexuality, generation, and connection are two of the themes that recur in Robbins's novels. The remaining five of the seven veils of *Skinny Legs and All* outline the other themes that Robbins favors in his work. The veils of political illusion, commerce, human omnipotence, Armageddon, and reliance on others must all be stripped away. People must understand that no one else will live life for them or take responsibility for them and that none of the other veils can be relied upon to care for the individual either. This view constitutes the seventh and final veil. Gurus, shamans, priests, and ministers can only point a direction for relating to the divine and the universe, but individuals must discern for themselves their role in the universe. The ultimate responsibility for life rests on oneself; no agency, religion, business, or political movement can tell people their way to live or to relate to reality and the divine. All must figure out for themselves their life's path; furthermore, no one else can step in and serve as a personal martyr or savior for the individual (*Skinny Legs* 468).

The illusion that money or commerce can serve as a guiding light for life's purpose disintegrates in Robbins's novels *Jitterbug Perfume* and *Half*

Asleep in Frog Pajamas. Although other themes are present in each of these novels, the false god of money dominates the lives of the major characters. In *Jitterbug Perfume,* characters pursue the secret base note of the greatest perfume. Each inventor wants to win the race of creativity and corner the market on the scent. In *Half Asleep,* the protagonist, Gwen Mati, believes financial success will erase her Filipina heritage and looks. With enough money, she will blend into the cultural climate of the United States. Her reliance on the stock market entices her into leveraging too much, and her career is ruined by a stock market crash. Gwen must regroup and in the process meets Larry Diamond, whom she regards as her one hope of averting the truth of her financial finagling being discovered on the following Monday. Diamond leads her into more self-analysis and exploration rather than providing her monetary salvation. The fifth veil of Salome's dance is the illusion of commerce as the secret of life.

A reliance on the judgment day is another illusion that humans must drop, according to Robbins's sixth veil. Ellen Cherry Charles's Uncle Buddy in *Skinny Legs* believes that the judgment day or Armageddon will bring righteous Christians to their just reward. All other religious faiths will perish. The belief in an afterlife and reward in the life after death is a control method exercised by religions and politics over believers. Robbins repeatedly voices the opinion that the belief in an afterlife is a cynical method that religions and governments use to force people into obedience and misery in the here and now. This view occurs primarily in *Skinny Legs, Another Roadside Attraction,* and *Even Cowgirls Get the Blues* but pervades all of Robbins's novels in one way or another.

The veil of political illusion is present in all of Robbins's novels also but plays its most important part in *Still Life with Woodpecker* and *Even Cowgirls Get the Blues.* Princess Leigh-Cheri in *Still Life* adores Ralph Nader, the political activist. She even attends a political meeting in Hawaii, joining thousands of environmentalists united for the cause. Bernard Mickey Wrangle, alias the Woodpecker, is an anarchist bomber who explains to Leigh-Cheri the tyranny of groups. Majority rule stifles the individual and discourages individual responsibility. Individuals no longer use their minds when they belong to political groups. The same sentiment occurs in *Even Cowgirls Get the Blues* when Delores Del Ruby rules the rebel cowgirls with the same tyranny that patriarchy uses. Delores and the radical cowgirls write a letter to the government authorities that Debbie and the more moderate cowgirls deem to be as pugnacious as the repressive system they are rebelling against. Robbins shows in the cowgirl rebellion that political movements that begin with good intentions often descend to petty tyranny that contradicts the initial impulse of the movement. Any institutionalization of politics or spirituality becomes controlling and kills the spirit. This third veil of political illusion supports the fourth veil of organized religion discussed above.

Both *Jitterbug* and *Half Asleep* contain characters who are trying to avoid death. Alobar and Larry Diamond, respectively, chase after immortality, introducing the theme of human omnipotence which is the second veil in *Skinny Legs*. Characters chasing the financial dream among characters chasing immortality blend nicely, since money is often regarded as a means of defeating death. Alobar and Larry Diamond realize that money is not the secret to longevity, but both pursue other illusions as their means of salvation. Alobar believes the return of Kudra, his true love, will save his life; Diamond believes the secret of Dr. Yamaguchi and the West African Bozos will provide a cure for his cancer. Ultimately these characters must make their own peace with the universe and with death.

The first veil of illusion is the evil of sexuality or the repression of the female. Blaming the female for all of the world's troubles creates tyranny and strife. Robbins suggests appreciation of the feminine spirit as the answer to the world's religious divisions and environmental disasters. It becomes a potent alternative to the world as people know it in Robbins's novels. Again, as discussed above in the section on characters and in the beginning of the section on themes, a return to the female principle as a guiding force of humanity promises a return to peace and happiness. Robbins's novels embrace the female as a positive, life-affirming energy. The feminine principle as a positive spirit populates each of Robbins's novels but predominates in *Another Roadside Attraction, Even Cowgirls Get the Blues, Skinny Legs and All,* and *Half Asleep in Frog Pajamas.* The answers to the secret of life reside in a celebration of female sexuality and the feminine. That celebration is life-enhancing and embracing.

The first veil returns readers to the seventh veil, which is a positive version of life that the individual must acknowledge on his or her own terms. No one can negotiate reality, spirituality, or creativity for anyone else. Once they do their own negotiating, people will live together in harmony because they will not try to force their view of reality or religion or sexuality on anyone else. Robbins does not suggest that this process of realization is easy or automatic or a magic potion that will instantly cure all of the world's problems. He does not simply offer Eastern philosophy to the West as the answer to the problems of the Occident but suggests a combination of the two views, based in a return to individual spirituality and expression that respects the female principle.

In addition to the themes already discussed, Robbins investigates objectification in his novels. *Still Life with Woodpecker* contains Robbins's extensive treatise on the signification of the object, specifically, the packaging of Camel cigarettes (162–69). The object has a state of being and a perspective, Robbins offers readers. The object has a life and people have relationships with objects. Continuing this theme further, Robbins presents animate inanimates as characters in *Skinny Legs and All*, the novel that follows *Still Life*. The spoon, can o'beans, sock, painted stick, and shell have voices, goals, and mobility. They also bring historical backgrounds with them, and they comment on human activities as they travel across the United States en route to Jerusalem and the ancient site of the goddess Astarte's temple. This life of objects is a natural extension of Robbins's comments on energy in his first novel, *Another Roadside Attraction*. All energy remains in the universe after a person or object dies or disintegrates; the energy does not leave, only the corporal body. Dinosaur energy remains floating in the universe after their extinction. This theory from physics informs much of Robbins's discussions about life, death, and existence. He imaginatively pursues this theory by applying it to objects. His characters, as do people generally, assign emotions and roles for objects, divining meaning from objects continually. Artists such as Andy Warhol and Claes Oldenburg are favorites of Robbins. Their artwork illustrates the beingness of objects. Robbins's excursion into the relationships of humans and "things" coalesces many of his themes— the interconnectedness of the world, the oppression of women via objectification, the negativity of religions that preach men's dominance of nature and all of the earth, and the killing of human spirituality that religion, politics, and business promote.

The novels of Tom Robbins shake readers out of complacency to a reevaluation of their values and choices. While promoting this introspection, Robbins's style of writing stretches the uses of language in positive and creative directions. His writing also plays games with the reader's imagination by expecting an acceptance of his novels' fantasy. Within the fantasy worlds of the novels, Robbins calls attention to the novel as a created text, an artwork that is constructed. The pose of reality in which fiction claims to be fact becomes regularly questioned in Robbins's self-exposing narrators. In addition to these philosophical and artistic challenges, humor and playfulness convey the joie de vivre that most readers appreciate in Robbins's novels. The Roman philosopher

Horace declared that the purpose of art was to instruct and entertain. Tom Robbins fulfills the qualifications of the master artist.

NOTES

1. Robbins had not read Vonnegut's books until after he finished writing his first novel. He copied the quotation from a journal article that had copied the quotation from Vonnegut without attribution. The sentiment in the passage appealed so much to Robbins that he in turn incorporated it as a comment by Bokonon in his novel. The story behind this incident is quite fascinating (see McCaffery and Gregory).

2. Thanks to Barbara Quigley, a student in my fall 1994 seminar on Tom Robbins, for her readings on the goddess in Robbins in her unpublished seminar paper, "Support of the Goddess Theory in Tom Robbins."

Another Roadside Attraction
(1971)

Tom Robbins conceived the premise for his first novel, *Another Roadside Attraction*, over the course of years as he was writing art reviews for the *Seattle Times*. Robbins quit the *Times* to try a year in New York City, believing it to be a center of art and a mecca for other experimenters with hallucinatory drugs. After returning to Seattle, he resumed reviewing and continued speculating about the consequences to the world and religion if a corpse of Jesus Christ was unearthed. One day during lunch at the Benjamin Franklin Hotel his host Luther Nichols, West Coast editor of Doubleday Books, asked him if he would like to write a book about West Coast artists. Instead Robbins declared that he was writing a novel and went home directly to begin recording on paper his speculations about the corpse of Jesus. In an interview, he shared that he had worked two years on planning the structure of *Another Roadside Attraction* (1971) (McCaffery and Gregory 231). Doubleday published 6,000 copies of the novel in hardback; the soft-cover rights were bought by Ballantine Books. With the success of his second novel, *Even Cowgirls Get the Blues*, people wanted to read *Roadside*, and it was successfully issued in paperback.

Besides the careful structure of the novel, Robbins's style, characters, themes, and manipulation of suspense via multiple texts capture a quintessentially 1960s perspective. The novel epitomizes life on the fringes of society during the 1960s. After analyzing the above elements of the novel, I will illustrate the method of analysis a Jungian psychological critic might use to discuss the novel's structure and characters.

PLOT DEVELOPMENT

Amanda meets John Paul Ziller, who has joined the Indo-Tibetan Traveling Circus with which she travels. John Paul's friend Plucky Purcell comes to the circus also, but while the group is sojourning up the West Coast of the United States to its various engagements, Plucky detours to perform an errand, never to rejoin the circus. In the meantime, John Paul and Amanda, after a circus wedding, stop along the road at an abandoned roadside restaurant. They stay and open a roadside zoo and wiener stand. The East Coast–trained scientist Marx Marvelous makes a pilgrimage to the roadside zoo looking for Amanda because he regards her as the priestess of modern spirituality. He is writing a comparative study of belief systems. He joins the Ziller family of John Paul; Amanda, her baby from a previous relationship, Baby Thor; and the baboon Mon Cul (whom the group liberated from life in a real zoo). His stay with the Zillers leads him to understand belief by discovering his own spiritual harmony with the intuitive. While the Ziller household settles into the zoo, they receive letters from Plucky Purcell, telling them about his adventures in a monastery of secret super spy monks. He ends up in the Vatican, where he discovers the corpse of Jesus Christ. Circumstances enable him to remove the corpse and send it to the Zillers. The FBI and several other security organizations track Plucky and the corpse to the zoo. The beginning of the novel is the end in which John Paul and Plucky have disappeared with the corpse, distracting their hunters from the zoo and leaving Amanda, Baby Thor, Mon Cul, and Marx Marvelous to deal only with the FBI.

Since the genre of the novel began as a story told in chronological order, readers notice that *Another Roadside Attraction* reverses custom and begins at the end. The presentation of this story seems nonlinear; that is, the narration does not progress in a straight chronological line. It circles around events, providing history when needed. Readers accumulate information pieces at a time and must connect what seem to be the multiple (nontraditional) plots of the Ziller's roadside zoo, Plucky Purcell's adventures, and Marx Marvelous's evolution into an integrated individual. Actually the story has one plot that is told incrementally and basically consists of these apparently three different plots. The plot follows the events leading up to the disappearance of John Paul Ziller and Plucky Purcell after Plucky recovers the corpse of Jesus Christ from the Vatican and brings it to the roadside zoo. The romance, marriage, and partnership of Amanda and John Paul, both formerly associated with the Indo-Tibetan Traveling Circus, are the essence of this novel; Plucky's adventures directly involve the Zillers. Therefore the multiple story lines of Plucky, Marx, Amanda, and John Paul revolve around a single plot. Because the universe is all connected, the adventures of these characters are all related to each others' experiences.

Robbins deliberately developed the circular narrative technique because he wanted to recreate an insider's experience of living with countercultural people during the 1960s. He is so successful that some reviewers have praised this novel as the best portrait of the sixties. Since part of that culture was experimenting with drugs, Robbins must create the hallucinatory aspect of taking LSD or cybercyllic mushrooms or marijuana. His search for a technique to convey not only the absurdities and profundities of drug use but also the spiritual quests of the sixties results in the concentric circles of the plot.

The circles of the plot illustrate the superiority of noninstitutional spirituality and of respectful harmony between humans and nature. Amanda and John Paul Ziller have reached a spiritual balance and equality. Outsiders must learn the value of nature, intuition, and spirit. The Plucky Purcell and Marx Marvelous stories propel the plot forward and serve to illustrate the philosophies of Amanda and John Paul. Purcell understands the Ziller philosophy, and Marx Marvelous must learn to accept the spiritual and appreciate Amanda's and John Paul's values.

At the center of the novel is the conjunction of all of the stories when Plucky Purcell arrives with the corpse and Marx Marvelous returns from a sojourn away from the roadside zoo. Everyone becomes involved with Plucky's discovery and the consequences of his acquisition of the corpse. With the existence of the corpse, the ascension becomes a myth that Christians, particularly Roman Catholics, have used as the basis of belief in God and Jesus. The entire religion is based on a hoax. No mystery remains of the religion if this elaborate early Christian trick becomes public. The zoo family must consider carefully the impact their knowledge may have on society. The plot develops to the point of this decision and its aftermath. The novel begins, however, with the end, the consequences of their decision.

Ambiguity about the living or dying of two central characters opens the book, leaving readers puzzled as to who these people are, why they are missing, and what has happened to them. The narrator reports that the Magician's underwear has been found in a cardboard suitcase in a pond on the fringes of Miami. The floating suitcase implies a plane crash, a boating accident, or a car accident. Some foul play is further suggested by the mention of Miami, known for its violence, its drug wars, and its Mafia. The opening sentence blends mystery with humorous earthiness and forces readers with any curiosity to continue reading.

Robbins sustains suspense and moves the plot further along. Readers continually have questions that they want answered in regard to Plucky Purcell's corpse escapades. Robbins satisfies and stimulates their curiosity with a series of letters from Purcell smuggled out of the monastery of super spy monks. Purcell's adventures involve the Ziller family with their concern for their friend. So as the Zillers establish their roadside zoo, they try to communicate with their friend and help him with his own adventure. The letters from Purcell to the Zillers integrate the love and mystery stories into one plot.

Besides the questions raised by the opening page of the novel, Robbins's foreshadowing at the ends of intervals further intrigues his readers as the suspense builds. The text has no chapter divisions, but has part divisions instead; foreshadowing therefore serves almost as chapter endings. One example of such a passage comes near the beginning of the narrative. Plucky Purcell has left the traveling circus because of another obligation and promises to join the group as soon as possible but does not because he shortly becomes the instigator of "the chain of events which was to put Amanda and John Paul Ziller in their present jeopardy, which was to threaten the well-being of millions, which was to lead to the drafting of this very report" (40). Such comments as the above compel readers to find out what Purcell has done that has placed the Zillers in danger. Calling the novel a "report" also suggests that the book is a document that is supposed to be factual rather than a story or a fiction. This pretense at fact interrupts the expected illusion of a realistic storytelling, jolting readers out of any sense of false security they may have. Novels are not supposed to refer to their process; readers have learned to expect seamless progressions from beginning to end. Robbins's insertion of the word "report," therefore, denies the "novelness" of the novel and influences readers into the acceptance of the story as fact. The comment does, however, provide more credibility because of its pose as a factual report. Events that we would dismiss as too fantastic or unrealistic may incline readers to abandon the novel, but the factual pretense keeps readers involved and willing to suspend their disbelief until the mystery of the missing persons is resolved. Most narratives would provide closure to the mystery that opens the novel as well as to the religious mystery that causes the disappearances. Robbins refuses such a tidy conclusion for the text.

To enhance the pretense of a report, Robbins has the narrator follow the foreshadowing of foul play to Plucky with "factual" information that readers traditionally want to know about characters. Earlier in the text Robbins even labels with a subtitle the information about Ziller's life as biographical notes that are subdivided again with Roman numerals. The pretense of fact continues with his treatment of Plucky. The passage about Plucky's nonappearance segues into a brief amusing scene with the newlyweds, Amanda and John Paul, and then returns to a biographical section about Plucky Purcell. The foray into the bonding of Amanda and John Paul inserts humor and absurdity into the serious events surrounding Plucky Purcell's failure to rejoin the circus. The lives of the lovers interrupt the chronological flow of information surrounding Plucky's delay. A further interruption to the Plucky story is the telling of Plucky's past which itself contains diversions into other information or incidents. In this manner Robbins continues to build suspense. This juxtaposition of the Ziller and Plucky events occurring simultaneously complicates the directness of the narrative and creates the illusion of circularity. Throughout the book, Robbins continues this moving from story to story, infusing the changes with foreshadowing. He also has Marx Marvelous interject comments about the task of writing the "report" and, as in many eighteenth- and nineteenth-century British novels, directly address the reader.

Robbins's interweaving of these various plot devices engenders complexity in a humorous novel that actually investigates the serious philosophical issues of spirituality, religious belief, values, and alienation. The plot sashays back and forth, riveting readers to the page to find out the results of Plucky and John Paul's disappearance and the end of the love story. Robbins refuses to finish the plot with a traditional ending and leaves readers with multiple ambiguities.

Robbins employs a third-person limited narration in *Another Roadside Attraction*. The narrator reports events and occasionally the unspoken reactions of the characters. The narrator reveals himself to be a participant in the events after he displays his identity to readers. The unidentified narrator weaves together the notebook of Marx Marvelous, the letters of Plucky Purcell, the journal of John Paul Ziller and the narrator's version of events past and present into a report. Since the third-person narrator dominates the text, it will come first in this discussion of point of view. The presentation of this narrator is also more complex than in the traditional novel's narration because it has a dual identity. The first identity is the unnamed third-person narrator, the second, Marx Marvelous as narrator. Because of this doubleness, readers must create two readings of the book once they understand that they are reading two books simultaneously: Marx Marvelous's as unnamed and Marx Marvelous's as scientist visitor to the Ziller compound.

Robbins plays with traditional narration in this book. Besides employing a third-person limited point of view, the author/narrator of the text addresses the reader directly and indicates his or her participation in the events that transpire. He breaks away from the story of the past and describes the present in which FBI agents have occupied the first floor of Amanda and John Paul Ziller's roadside zoo. The switching from past to present adds to the circular nature of the narration. When the narrator switches to the present events, he self-consciously mentions his role and performance as recorder.

The writer of the texts we are reading poses as a reporter by calling himself a correspondent, suggesting he is reporting the news. The pose encourages the belief that the events being reported are receiving the objective treatment that the news media is reputed to offer. Once Marx Marvelous admits that he is the reporter (224), all of the previous news must be read as the subjective account that it is.

Marx Marvelous is actually the third-person narrator/writer of the text, but he does not reveal his authorship until after he has grown worthy of sex with Amanda. His sexual initiation has a counterpart in his near drowning. Marx undergoes a symbolic baptism and rebirth as a whole human being. Instead of being dominated by logic, he combines scientific logic with an openness to intuition and spirituality. Marx is a participant in the story and consequently not objective about the people and events he shares. He is an unreliable narrator, an untrustworthy reporter, whose disclosure of involvement forces readers to reread and reevaluate all of the earlier material in the book. The concept of the unreliable narrator describes a narrator who tells a story with his or her own self-interest involved. The person may be guilty of a crime or indiscretion and explains her or his culpability by slanting the tale in a flattering, self-pitying, or ingenuous voice. Marx Marvelous poses as the anonymous author pretending objectivity. When we reread or if we are "careful readers," to quote Marvelous, we accumulate enough hints to surmise that the author is Marvelous before he reveals himself. This knowledge increases the reader's enjoyment of Marvelous's self-referential comments throughout the narration. An example of his self-interest and self-consciousness as a narrator is the update of the situation in the roadside zoo. The excerpt provides clues to the identity of the reporter simply because Marvelous is the only male left in the zoo, unless the narrator is an as yet unidentified member of the zoo family. The reporter writes about Amanda's inquiries into his activities and his attempts to record these events:

> He did not, of course, tell her that it was *she* who was the substance of his accounting. To reveal that would be to reveal the breadth of his esteem for her—which she would consider excessively misplaced in light of the Corpse, who, dead as it was, was the true and important protagonist in this drama. (44)

Clearly, then, the individual reporting events is someone not only on the scene, but someone with a desire to portray Amanda as marvelous herself. The reporter does not hide his bias; readers simply must guess at his identity. The "author," as he calls himself, conceals his attraction for Amanda out of respect for her turmoil and her devotion to her missing husband, John Paul Ziller. That Marvelous's focus is on Amanda, who is his redeemer, rather than on the corpse of Jesus Christ means that Marvelous's narration must portray the marvels of Amanda. One example of a marvel is the episode about Amanda's butterfly preservation effort which not only displays her vast knowledge but also her appreciation of nature. As befitting a redeemer, she learns never to kill or confine animals. When she contemplates the possible contents of her roadside zoo, this lesson informs her decision.

Passages such as Amanda's presentation on butterflies are reminiscent of Herman Melville's "Cetology" chapter in *Moby Dick*. They lack the elaborateness of detail but contain the weight of the accretion of material in Melville's chapters. The sections of philosophical discussions have a similar feeling. As in reading Melville, readers of Robbins must pause to integrate these informative passages into the flow of humor and narrative. Readers may dismiss these passages as interruptions that have nothing to do with the development of character or narrative, but they are wrong if they do so; indeed, these passages have integral roles in each chapter. The butterfly passage demonstrates Amanda's extensive knowledge of the lepidoptera and illustrates Amanda's intelligence. She is a naturalist who merges her intellectual understanding with an intuitive chthonic appreciation and identification with the natural. Therefore, such passages forward rather than divert the plot.

In self-praise that grows in irony, the narrator is also capable of praising himself. He refuses false modesty but jokes about his superiority. His self-presentation, then, employs the arrogance that he had before he discovers his intuitive self. He is capable after the discovery of his intuitive side of using humorous irony about his hubris. He achieves this self-knowledge by recognizing that his intuitive side is as important as his intellectual side. Amanda leads him through the riddles, meditations, and tests necessary to attain this inner balance and harmony. His narration, then, must be read at two levels: the initial third-person narrative and the self-reflective first-person narrative that the first reading actually becomes once Marx Marvelous reveals his role as narrator.

The self-conscious narration supplies clues throughout the first two-thirds of the book to the identity of the writer if the reader pays attention. Identifications such as "this writer" and "your reporter" call attention to the writing process as well as to the person recording the events. Rather than being space fillers or distractions, these apparent interruptions to the text wrench readers away from a comfortable illusion of art as reality and force them to consider questions such as the identity of the author, the narrator, and the construction of each phenomenon as fictive. Readers, therefore, cannot confuse the words of any of the characters, narrator, or author as representative of Tom Robbins, the person creating the entire illusion of the text as a journal or report on the events of the narrator's summer with the Zillers' menagerie. Using the narrator's interruptions as a means of directly talking to readers about the writing process, Robbins reminds readers that all history recorders have their own agenda and biases. By making Marx Marvelous the primary narrator and by interjecting letters and journal entries from other characters, Robbins distances himself from the text. Besides creating distance from the text, the multiple points of view in the novel provide information that Marvelous would not have ordinarily known.

CHARACTERS

Some reviewers complain that Robbins's characters are never developed or fully rounded characters (Peters 72). In *Another Roadside Attrac-*

tion this critical complaint is correct. Characters are representative of types rather than rounded characters that actually develop. Amanda is most often described as an earth goddess or mother goddess. As critics' and the narrator's most discussed character, she embodies the most potent mythological and psychological type. Because of her symbolic nature, she remains flat. Amanda is nineteen at the novel's opening. Although her father is mentioned, no mother appears in the novel. Amanda is part Puerto Rican and part Anglo.

John Paul Ziller is the quintessential caveman. Among his characteristics are his unintelligible utterances alternating with philosophical eloquence, his BMW motorcycle, his drumming expertise, and his loincloth costume. He is the completely natural man with a high degree of creativity in his art. In contrast to John Paul, Marx Marvelous personifies the modern man of science or the completely unnatural man. He is so alienated from nature that walking in the rain makes him wince (133–34). His research into modern religious faith and forms of spirituality is from a psychological and empirical perspective rather than intuitive or spiritual. The other primary male character in the novel is Plucky Purcell, who represents the American hero. He is an ex–football star who was a "natural" athlete destined for NFL greatness. He is a southern aristocrat whose family has settled downward into the lower middle class. As an all-American male, his career ends when the backfield coach discovers an affair between Purcell and the coach's wife. He joins the Navy officers training school, only to be kicked out again for misdemeanors. His career then becomes one of an altruistic criminal who connects women with safe abortionists and sells nonnarcotic drugs to artists. He is a socially responsible criminal, but still all-American because he relates to Amanda as a sexual piece of meat when he first meets her.

Nearly Normal Jimmy serves as a voice throughout the narrative. Although his actual appearance as a character ends when the Indo-Tibetan circus leaves the Zillers and Purcell, his role as ringmaster for the circus extends to ringmaster of life as far as the Zillers, Purcell, and eventually Marx Marvelous are concerned. The characters frequently refer to a statement Nearly Normal has made about life. Nearly Normal becomes a wise voice that speaks from offstage, directing the characters in their decisions and actions. He serves as a god figure and the characters refer to him the way Christians quote the Bible as the word of God, a disembodied voice. Other characters constantly in the narrative, but playing smaller parts are Baby Thor, Amanda's child from an earlier love affair, who has electric eyes and is named after the principal Norse god (represented by thunder), and Mon Cul, prince of baboons and John Paul Ziller's beloved companion.

Although all of the male characters have last names, Amanda, the primary focus of the novel, is never identified with a surname. We are told twice that her father is quite fat, but he is not named. This focus on Amanda as a one-name phenomenon like a movie star or rock star or prophetess contributes to her character's being a symbol rather than a rounded character with depth created in the usual manner by a full name and history. At nineteen Amanda believes life has three purposes, birth, copulation, and death (8). She speaks in cryptic sentences, quite often asking questions that are unanswerable or are puzzles like Zen koans (4, 5). Amanda also believes in seeking nontraditional cures for illness and practices Eastern and Native American philosophy, seeking answers in nature and spirituality. Her characterization is best expressed in the words of BaBa, the toadstool visionary: "Logic only gives man what he needs . . . Magic gives him what he wants" (7). Amanda's attractiveness resides in her mystery. She combines earthiness—picking mushrooms, cooking and brewing concoctions of herbs, roots, and vegetables—with spirituality—meditating alone in the woods for forty days, nurturing animals and humans, tuned into lightning and energy forms. She is an earth mother goddess and a Christ figure who redeems humans from their slavery to logic. After Marx Marvelous reaches his understanding, Amanda permits him to have sex with her; his rebirth finishes with Mon Cul saving him from nearly drowning. As a result, he becomes a whole person and identifies himself as having been the narrator of the novel all along, in case readers have missed the hints of his viewpoint and voice. Amanda has been his vehicle of change.

Even though Marx Marvelous asserts that Amanda is the focus of his report, her cryptic wisdom becomes secondary to Marx Marvelous's self-exploration. Marx is the mirror through which Amanda's philosophy is reflected as it helps him reconcile the logical and intuitive sides of himself. His observations and interactions with Amanda teach him about living in harmony with the masculine (reason and logic) and feminine (emotion and nature) sides of himself.

For a discussion of Marx Marvelous as narrator, the reader should consult the point of view section in this chapter. Marvelous's traits as a character reveal themselves in his self-descriptions and in the entries from others' letters and journals. In the commentary that Marvelous makes about Amanda's discovering his task as self-appointed chronicler of the Ziller-Purcell mystery, Marvelous does reveal that Amanda is the most important feature of his report. While writing about the disappearance of Plucky and John Paul, Marx expresses his feelings about Amanda and his situation. He shows his chagrin at Amanda's "belatedly" noticing his occupation. Presumably she has been worrying about her missing husband and his friend Plucky rather than attending to Marx (44). Readers studying the passage learn more about the narrator's personality or adopted persona for the earlier portion of the novel than they learn about Amanda. He feels unappreciated because Amanda has not noticed him writing earlier. In addition, he assumes humility and guilt about his "esteem" for Amanda since Christ, the corpse, would strike most people as more important than a spiritual hippie teen-aged girl. His comments suggest a self-conscious desire on the part of him, the reporter, to write well with a higher level of vocabulary.

Whenever Marx Marvelous chooses to educate the reader, his didacticism in passages such as the biological information about butterflies is inoffensive because these parts are interrupted by humorous comments about the speaker, the audience, or the narrator. His portrait of Amanda in the butterfly passage illustrates not only Amanda's vast knowledge of biology but also Marx Marvelous's appreciation of Amanda's philosophy at this time. He describes the characters in her audience as misfits being entertained whereas Amanda is serious about her efforts to know and share her appreciation of butterflies. She is not interested in the Latin names of the species as Madame Goody is, but rather Amanda focuses on the characteristics and beauty of the insect.

STYLE

When Marx Marvelous confesses his role as narrator, he acknowledges that his "report" has a "broken pace" with "contradictions," "vagueness," "digressions," and a "thousand and one shifts in style" (224). He explains these "stylistic inconsistencies" as "the natural state of Cancerians." Amanda reassures Marx that his astrological sign indicates an easily influenced personality. Parts of his text, therefore, "turn out written in John Paul Ziller's idiom, parts in Plucky Purcell's idiom and parts of the idiom of the young mistress of the zoo" (225). Robbins ends this sentence with a challenge question that a reader might find in a child's picture book: "(can you pick out those parts where each holds sway?)." To round off this list of parts, Robbins has Marvelous add that "there

are times when everybody talks alike and that is like a smart-assed doctor of philosophy candidate at Johns Hopkins U." (225). The remark, of
course, is self-referential and refers directly to Marx Marvelous, the
"smart-assed" doctoral candidate from Johns Hopkins. All of this mixture of language styles corresponds to the different voices that speak in
the narrative. It also parallels the abrupt jumps in action from one person's story or from one time or place to another.

In addition to using the ridiculous situations that characters experience
and their respective voices, Robbins creates humor with his unconventional language use. Robbins's style blends slang and an occasional swear
word, if the character would use it, with sophisticated philosophical and
technical language. This pairing of colloquial and nonsense words with
a sophisticated vocabulary often creates humor and usually surprises the
reader. Blending the extremes of language parallels the mixing of humor
and serious philosophy which occurs in the novel. Furthermore, Robbins
creates words of his own and uses nonsense sounds. He has characters
talk in riddles and writes of personal body functions, eliminative and
sexual, as perfectly common items in the narration. Puns or playing on
the meanings or sounds of words create gentle amusement in Robbins's
works and emphasize the text's joyfulness. Further elements of Robbins's
style are his use of figurative language such as similes and metaphors,
that is, comparisons using "like" or "as," or comparisons that replace
the item with a word suggesting the comparison without using "like"
or "as." The classic examples of these two figurative styles are: My love
is like a red red rose (simile) and My love is a rose (metaphor).

Robbins's pairing of serious issues with frivolous metaphors and similes occurs frequently in the novel. When Marx Marvelous announces his
role as narrator, he describes his subject of the second coming of Christ
or the never-ever leaving of Christ from this Earth as a task that could
be never ending because the Corpse could resurface at any time:
"(. . . for even as I type these words the returned Christ might be revealing himself to the cameras on some strip of Florida sand where
heretofore only citrus cuties in bikinis may have posed—and can the
shock of world recognition be far behind)?" (224). In this passage, Robbins puns on the multiple meanings of "revealing himself." Furthermore,
he juxtaposes the holy figure of Christ and "citrus cuties in bikinis,"
completing the ironies with the formal academic usage of "heretofore."
Creating even more irony, Marx describes himself, after his sketch of
Christ's possible manifestation, as an "admittedly ambivalent boy scientist to whom the true and powerful workings of language remain a

puzzle" (224). Of course, Marx Marvelous's narration reveals the contrary; he is an adept user of language.

Since all levels of language comprise Robbins's style, the narration includes the use of several slang words for sexual activities and body parts. Most of these arise in discourses about Amanda when the narrative is not otherwise delineating action or philosophical dilemmas. The men mostly relate to Amanda as sex object, and Robbins represents this attitude with descriptions in slang of Amanda's sexual parts and the men's overt sexual responses. Robbins's control of the language and description creates a tone of normality about sex. His treatment of the sexual is not coy but matter-of-fact. Since Western male literature has traditionally concentrated on the female as sex object, Robbins's text adds to the tradition by including references to the male's physical sexual responses. Readers react to these scenes with a degree of comfort or discomfort depending upon their learned conditioning toward sex. A reader who has absorbed the message that sex is dirty or bad will probably react with anger, embarrassment, outrage, or giggles. If the reader resists the lessons that sex is to be hidden, she or he will most likely react with equanimity. Both, however, may be shocked by the language because few are accustomed to sex publicly discussed in such language unless they lived during the 1960s and associated with so-called countercultural people. Since the sexual aggressiveness and dehumanizing of such slang remain predominant in the culture, the sixties attempts at neutralizing the negative connotation of the language failed.

The results of the counterculture's style in Robbins are a text full of surprising and startling combinations of thought, image, and language in a mixture of whimsy, humor, speculations on life and its purpose, and explorations of belief and spirit.

THEME

Another Roadside Attraction overflows with themes to explore. The best is probably the "Great Purpose of Life" or the nature of belief, which includes the necessity of magic as well as logic in life, the unity of all life, the needed tolerance of difference, the tyranny of organized religion, and the life force as never-ending energy. The creation of human life and earth is the "Infinite Goof" that Heissenberg's "Uncertainty Principle" dominates (215).

The characters in the novel search in their different ways for answers to the question of the purpose of life, science, and art. Amanda explores this question by talking to a variety of people. She asks a Navaho sand painter, who creates sacred ceremonial images, what the function of art is. Amanda also asks a group of gypsies to identify her true nature. They reply that she is an inquisitive person. Amanda speaks with a priest. Instead of enlightening her, he demands of her the nature of her beliefs. She believes in magic and freedom. Furthermore, Amanda continually seeks insight via the ingesting of various substances and falling into trances. She and the other characters epitomize the 1960s drug use and other alternative philosophies as methods to expand their minds and search for deeper insights into themselves and life. They were not escaping but delving into life.

In ways similar to Amanda's, John Paul Ziller has explored his mind and the world, particularly Africa or India. Ziller and Amanda agree that "In our human cells are recorded every single impulse of energy that has occurred since the beginning of time" (50). The "DNA genetic system" is a "library" to "browse" in for John Paul (50–51). He uses for access various methods such as the vegetable and meditative, among others. Death poses a minimum of fear because John Paul and Amanda believe that death is a dispersal of a person's energy.

This energy theory introduces the portrayal of life as a universal oneness. Marx Marvelous observes and then imitates Amanda and John Paul's acceptance of nature. They do not try to avoid rain, but rather they welcome the rain and walk calmly through it, receiving it as a necessary element of life (133–34). Harmony with nature pervades the novel as the characters repeatedly learn from various animals and vegetables the connectedness of all life.

This awareness of unity with all life grows in Amanda and John Paul. When the Zillers consider the contents of their zoo, Amanda realizes with shame that her earlier period of collecting butterfly specimens was unnecessarily cruel and destructive. The butterfly represents to her the essence of beauty. "All the problems of art" are solved for Amanda by her chance observation of a special butterfly (226). The butterfly represents another instance of the unity of life. Robbins uses the physics theory that every movement or thought has an impact around the world. The flutter of a butterfly's wings affects the flow of air around the world. The theory also asserts that a thought in one part of the world can be part of a universal thought energy so that people on opposite sides of the globe can be developing the same theory simultaneously.

Nearly Normal has conducted his own explorations for the secret of life. He believes that the Dalai Lama in Tibet knows the secret of life. When he leaves John Paul and the circus, he heads for Tibet to be the projectionist for the Dalai Lama, showing him Marx Brothers movies. Here Robbins alludes to one of the epigraphs at the novel's beginning which in turn refers to a passage from Lowell Thomas's *Out of this World*, "What to Take When You Go to Tibet." The monks in Tibet would not want to watch movies that show killing, Thomas assumes. Therefore, humor, as in the Marx Brothers movies, and the romance of the jungle, as in Tarzan movies, are the appropriate elements for entertainment. Exiled from Tibet in 1959, the Dalai Lama would not have been at home when Nearly Normal arrived. Consequently, Robbins enriches the humor of the scene with irony.

Nearly Normal Jimmy's belief in the wisdom of the Dalai Lama and his followers reinforces the novel's premise that organized religion is deadly to the human imagination and spirit. Furthermore, organized religion operates for profit, and Christianity represented as the Catholic Church bases its existence on a lie. Plucky's discovery of the corpse of Jesus Christ proves that Christianity is a hoax. The zoo family decides not to reveal their discovery about Catholicism because they believe nothing in the world would change because of this revelation. Their view results from Plucky's understanding that religions and governments exist for profit. His adventures in the monastery and the Vatican reinforce his disillusionment in organized institutions. Nearly Normal Jimmy has anticipated Purcell's discovery and already fled to Tibet. To Nearly Normal the monks of Tibet know the secret of life and have shared it with the rest of the world. Governments have tried to eliminate this information by outlawing LSD. Amanda suggests to Nearly Normal that the coincident appearance of LSD and China's invasion of Tibet is not kismet. This group of Buddhists seems to have a belief system that is truly not for profit.

A respect for nature extends to a respect for all people no matter how different they are. This acknowledgment of people's value extends to equality for women and minorities. An example of this equality is the nature of the Zillers' marriage. They are partners in the manner in which they handle Plucky Purcell's return to the zoo with the corpse from the Vatican. As equals, the zoo family ponders individually the implications of Jesus Christ's corpse existing instead of disappearing as Bible stories tell readers. Then they all congregate to discuss and negotiate their plans for the corpse. Amanda expresses their respect for all human beings when she disagrees with her father's opinion that she is spending too

much time with weird people. She replies that people are not weird;
some simply need more understanding.

ALTERNATE READING: A JUNGIAN
INTERPRETATION

Carl Jung expanded his studies of the human mind by joining disciples
of Freud. Freud and Jung were close friends, and Jung for years a member of the inner circle of Freud's followers. Eventually believing that
Freud concentrated too much on controlling the methods of his followers, Jung broke from Freud in pursuit of his own approach to the human
mind. He is known as the founder of analytic psychology based on his
premise that there are two parts to the human unconscious: the personal,
containing the repressed experiences of the individual, and the archetypal, being part of the collective unconscious. His theories focused on
common spiritual and mythic elements in all cultures or the collective
unconscious.

Jung developed the idea that all humans in all cultures share a psychic
collective unconscious. All people carry deep in their minds common
spiritual, emotional, and mental patterns and symbols. Jung investigated
shared symbols and myths across cultures. His research led him to develop categories of archetypes or types of personalities that are found in
all societies. The archetypes rely on mythic symbols that Jung discovered
during his comparative studies.

Followers of Jung's ideas applied his theories to different fields such
as art, religion, and literature. Joseph Campbell wrote many books about
the shared myths and spirituality of humans, continuing Jung's work.
Vladimir Propp wrote a comparative study of myth and literary plots
based on his findings of a fixed number of story lines throughout cultural
myths. Northrop Frye found a set number of literary archetypes of stories, two examples of which are that texts are tragic or comic. Stories,
therefore, have at their roots shared spiritual myths.

Tom Robbins did graduate study in philosophy and religion and still
reads journals on Eastern philosophy (Interview 1994). Interpreting *Another Roadside Attraction* from a Jungian perspective harmonizes with
Robbins's background, but most importantly it illuminates a text that
employs spiritual archetypes.

Jungian psychologists and critics such as Frye believe that narratives
follow the patterns of the collective unconscious. Not only do the stories

illustrate universal patterns; the characters also represent certain classic archetypes of traits and values. A Jungian critic would interpret Amanda, for instance, as the archetype of the earth mother goddess. She continually seeks shelter in the woods or on hills during thunder and lightning storms. She also represents fertility, having given birth once and been pregnant twice (the second fetus miscarries after she falls in the woods). She also is the channel for Marx Marvelous's rebirth as an integrated individual. Amanda consults with spirits in the atmosphere and is a vehicle for their self-expression when she goes into trances. Amanda is an expert on butterflies and mushrooms. She can survive in the woods for forty days. She is characterized by Nearly Normal Jimmy "as a religion-unto-herself" (140). Her meditations in the woods for forty days may remind readers of Jesus Christ's forty days of meditation and temptation. The characterizations of Amanda reinforce her spiritual and sexual potency. Like a mother goddess she rewards her warriors or solaces them with a sexual encounter, after they have earned their privilege. The Jungian critic would proceed in analyzing the other characters and events in the book as further archetypes.

The book itself fits a Jungian vision of the world in its organization. The opening that is the ending resembles in mythic interpretations the euroboric snake, which holds its tail in its mouth, signifying that the end is the beginning forever through life. Life is a never-ending circle. No one can separate the beginning or ending of a story because each attempt to find a source leads to another story. Each ending is the beginning of the story. Beginning at the end, then, creates curiosity about the story and offers a clear indication that this story is on a mythic scale. The ambiguity of the floating articles of Plucky Purcell and John Paul Ziller suggests their possible deaths or their possible reappearances. The story presents archetypal heroes who have gone in quest of a holy grail, the secret of life, and spirituality. A Jungian critic would analyze these characters according to their contributions to the action of the plot and the imagery associated with them.

Another Roadside Attraction can be read as a perspective of the 1960s and as an archetypal text of mythic proportions. These approaches combine to elucidate this novel as about local and universal concerns. The archetypal nature of the book presents the sixties as an earnest period in history when people, young and old, were reevaluating the nature of spirituality, belief, and government. The Vietnam War is a constant in the background and sometimes in the foreground of the book. The hate from the War is counterbalanced by people who reject that hate and believe that all life forms should be respected. The flower children of the sixties celebrated life amidst much questioning and exploring of alternatives to the military-industrial complex that President Dwight Eisenhower so aptly identified. *Another Roadside Attraction*, to paraphrase Henry Fielding, is a "comic-tragic-epic poem in prose" (Preface: *The History of Tom Jones* 1749). It deserves to be enjoyed for its comedy and pondered for its philosophy.

4

Even Cowgirls Get the Blues
(1976)

Tom Robbins's second novel was an immediate success. Fans of his first novel, *Another Roadside Attraction*, were anticipating *Even Cowgirls Get the Blues*. Robbins's agent, Phoebe Larmore, convinced Houghton Mifflin that issuing *Cowgirls* simultaneously in hardback and paperback would create a marketing success. She was right. In less than a month, the hardback was in a second printing; the paperback version went through nine printings between March and October 1976. Bantam Books followed Houghton Mifflin in 1977, issuing another three printings of the paperback during that year.

Scholars have written more critical analyses of this second novel, *Even Cowgirls Get the Blues*, than any of his other five novels. Robbins uses both the road novel and the Western cowpoke genres, both of which involve the main character in a coming of age. That is, the character faces a test of courage that results in maturity or attainment of psychological assimilation and independence. The "road" formula conforms to the quest motif from stories of the knights seeking the Holy Grail. A contemporary analog is Jack Kerouac's *On the Road*. The Western motif fits with cowboy movies and novels such as *Shane*. Frederick Karl and Marc Siegel, respectively, categorize *Cowgirls* as a cowboy myth novel. Additionally, Karl reads *Cowgirls* as a bildungsroman or a novel of growing up (168). Traditionally, males have been the protagonists on the road, on the quest, or in a shoot-out. Until recently the majority of bildungsromane featured the story of a male maturing. Robbins develops his own variations on these classic formulae, using females for the heroes.

The major themes of this novel are toleration of difference, self-acceptance, and freedom. Encompassed within these themes are women's particular need for freedom and self-acceptance. In addition society needs to practice toleration. Robbins uses the protagonist Sissy Hankshaw to illustrate the importance of these values. Sissy possesses beauty, courage, and oversized thumbs. Instead of being saddened by her enormous thumbs, she accepts them as they are and uses them for their strengths as hitchhiking tools. When Sissy contorts herself into society's expectations of the female by becoming married to Julian Gitche, she loses her sense of self in efforts to be "normal." Somehow Sissy must reconcile her need for freedom and self-acceptance with her other needs for love and societal endorsement. Societal toleration for her unusual thumbs and her hitchhiking vocation would give Sissy the freedom she needs to express her true nature to the fullest. Society, however, has difficulty in letting Sissy be herself.

Cowgirls is a novel about toleration for individual difference. Characters in the book face several tests of their ability to encounter people or situations that the mainstream would find "not normal." Most of the characters endorse this individuality; those who do not fail to achieve more than mediocrity in their lives. Because of the characters' calm regarding abnormalities, readers accept more readily the idiosyncrasies of the Chink, the Countess, and Sissy. Other differences that society fails to accept are female cattle managers (cowgirls), Native Americans, non-materialists, and homosexuals. When the cowpokes of the Rubber Rose refuse to be cowpokes for "show" (they had expected to be managing a cattle ranch), the book's sympathy and admiration endorse them for their resourcefulness. Moreover, Robbins writes of the lesbian encounters of Sissy and the cowgirls as sexual expression and the pursuit of love. Sissy's adventures on and off the road are lessons for the reader as well as the character. Tolerance for difference enables people to embrace themselves as they are without mutilating their bodies or their personalities to suit society's concept of beauty or normality. Tolerance also allows people to exercise freedom. Therefore, this theme serves as an umbrella that creates the atmosphere for the other themes to flourish.

Other themes of the book include the need for moderation in one's views and life, the oppression of nature and of women, and the arbitrariness of concepts that people think are normal and fixed such as time and the proper size of thumbs. The book accretes layers of incidents illustrating these concepts, moving from major to minor character and back up to major characters to solidify Robbins's themes.

PLOT DEVELOPMENT

The plot of *Even Cowgirls Get the Blues* does not move in a direct chronological order. The book moves from the present to the past and from one location to another where events are happening simultaneously. The juxtapositions of action in New York and the Rubber Rose recall the device of cartoons, old Saturday radio plays, and television shows that announce, "Meanwhile at the okay corral...". Robbins identifies these switches in setting as "interludes," as in "Cowgirl Interlude (Bing)" (103), and "Cowgirl Interlude (Moon over Dakota)" (68). In the later part of the novel, Robbins indicates this same narrative shifting by icons shaped suspiciously like teeth or vulvas (see 241–44). These shifts in location, the contrast between high and low art, the multiplicity of Sissy's lovers create extremes that Beverly Gross calls the essence of the novel: "The novel *is* its unbridgeabilities," according to Gross (38). The narrative structure sets up and then bridges these extremes.

After Sissy travels from the Dakotas back to New York, the novel maintains a linear plot structure. Reports of the Rubber Rose come to Sissy and the reader via letters from Bonanza Jellybean. Robbins does, however, maintain the reporting of simultaneous events or thoughts of characters when they are separated. After the background information that readers need is complete, the plot essentially proceeds in the traditional chronological form.

One could describe *Cowgirls* as the first novel that features a female protagonist who exemplifies Joseph Campbell's concept of the "hero of a thousand faces." This description encompasses the hero of the road novel, the Grail quest, and the cowboy myth because these plot lines include Campbell's hero searching for an abstraction often unclear to the hero herself. Traditionally the hero must face obstacles to her self-discovery. Sometimes the obstacles are people who symbolize certain traits she finds seductive and must reject. Other times the hero faces physical threats that she must defeat.

The plot of *Even Cowgirls Get the Blues* includes the classic elements of these hero myths. Among the threats Sissy must confront are her family's shame over her thumbs. The family's reactions threaten acceptance of herself and her point of view. The successive humiliations Sissy suffers because her family refuses to accept her thumbs test her self-respect and determination. She resists the social rejection of her giantism and thrives. Her uncle's comment that hitchhiking was the only use for her thumbs is meant as a joke. Toddler Sissy takes his comment seriously and begins practicing thumb moves for her future career. Therefore, Sissy as hero starts in the cradle with her resistance to the worries her family has about normalcy.

Years later her mother's consultation with the "spiritualist" about Sissy's prospects for a husband registers at a deep level in the teenaged girl. This tinge of self-doubt that she absorbs leads her to act out her mother's dream. Consequently her marriage to Julian Gitche evokes a desire for normalcy and poses even a physical threat to Sissy. Sissy's wish to be "normal" for Julian and her fear of her thumbs' power to hurt (after her attack on the Countess) lead her to surgery on her oversized thumbs. This test of her inner strength sends her back to the Dakotas, hitchhiking all the way, and renewing her trust in herself. The pressures from Julian, Dr. Goldman, and the Countess to conform send her out of her centeredness and into a violence she has never exerted before. Their demands push her into self-mutilation as a reaction to the powerful force her thumbs possess and to her discovery of the darker side of herself. Because her thumbs ache and hurt so much after the surgery, she listens to them again and realizes nothing more needs to change. She restores herself to herself by heading West rather than staying in the East with the forces that endorse unnaturalness or self-alienation.

When Sissy arrives back at the Rubber Rose Ranch, she stumbles onto a violence that assumes a life of its own. The cowgirls have challenged the authorities over the protection and possession of the whooping cranes. The aggressive authorities prove to be such a monolith of power and violence that the cowgirls' surrender cannot stop the escalation of tension and anger that the law enforcement officers harbor. The traditional shoot-out at the ranch of Western cowboy novels ensues. Sissy cannot enter the ranch property and consequently detaches herself from the group and the situation. She joins the Chink in the hills to be cured of her self-alienation and depression over the Rubber Rose deaths and damage. When the Chink moves on to further places, Sissy remains as a sign of hope for the future. Her pregnancy embodies the chance of the future generation learning self-knowledge and unity with the universe.

The narrative point of view of *Cowgirls* consists of a third-person omniscient narrator. This narrator can tell readers the thoughts and motivations of any characters. In contrast to *Another Roadside Attraction*, the *Cowgirls* narrator is not a major character participating in the plot. Robbins creates a persona for the narrative voice. Readers must be aware that the narrative point of view in a book is not necessarily reflective of the author's self or beliefs. To confuse any readers who may make this equation, Robbins introduces the character Dr. Robbins, a psychiatrist at a New York clinic. Additionally, Robbins creates the Chink, who is sought after as the authority on life. Robbins establishes several voices that exhibit an authority readers usually like to equate with the author's view. Therefore readers must decide for themselves which voice is the author's position on issues. Robbins illustrates with his manipulation of the omniscient narrator the premise of the novel: everyone has to figure out life individually; no one can do it for anyone else.

To emphasize Robbins's view, the narration moves among the thoughts of the characters. The plot movements from one location to another are really leaps from one character's mind to another's. The reports of facts that readers receive, consequently, are from the perspective of the character or the narrator. In *Cowgirls*, the male narrator calls himself "the author." "He" intrudes into the reporting of events and comments on his task. Robbins uses the playwright and theorist Bertolt Brecht's alienation technique, which Brecht developed as a corrective to the complacency of bourgeois theater. An example of this technique occurs whenever "the author" intrudes into the text with an observation. The persona of the narrator/author reports his opinion about Dr. Goldman's judgment of Sissy's paean to hitchhiking: "The author frankly doesn't know. The author isn't altogether certain that there is any such thing as exaggeration" (55). Robbins has the author continue his monologue as a dialogue uniting the reader with the author by the use of the first-person plurals "we" and "our." Robbins establishes the illusion of a conversation between the author and the reader, thereby involving the reader as part of the novel's consciousness. Furthermore, Robbins invokes the reader's perceptions to help the reader empathize with the author's response to Goldman's declaration that Sissy exaggerates: "Suppose you awoke one morning with the uneasy feeling that the world had . . . somehow slipped a-tilt" (55). Suddenly the omniscient narrator reads the mind of the reader, moving beyond the limits of the facade of so-called reality and reminding readers that they too are part of the illusion of truth that a story pretends. The alienation from the text as truth keeps them aware of the illusion. The reader colludes with the writer/narrator in the success of the fiction.

Robbins's defamiliarization techniques stretch to create another voice which orders the author/narrator around in the text. When Robbins introduces the whooping cranes into the text, he creates another persona that directs the author persona. This boss voice orders the author to write a description of the cranes and awards the preferred passage a grade. This chapter continues until the over-voice grades a final effort an acceptable B (179–80). Just in case the reader has become complacent with the author persona, Robbins removes reliability from the author. Again the reader becomes aware of the illusion of fact. In many interviews, Robbins repeats his stance as a romantic. He refuses the label "realism," even though his books overflow with encyclopedic information. Robbins shows that facts coexist with fantasy and that some people's reality may be fantasy based on facts. The persistent wrenching of the reader away from a mindless reliance on the author/narrator makes point of view a key method of holding the reader's attention and interest in the novel.

The final irony of the book is Robbins's announcement at the end of the novel that Dr. Robbins is the one who gathered all of the material for the story. The Dr. Robbins character, however, does not interact with the narrative as much as Marx Marvelous does in *Another Roadside Attraction*. He remains a character described with the same omniscient third-person style as the other characters. His actions and influence are primarily offstage.

CHARACTERS

The primary characters of the novel are in their own ways social outsiders. As Beverly Gross points out, Robbins's "central message" is that "In an overstructured world only the misfit is free" (36). Sissy's thumbs mark her as different from other people. Julian Gitche is on the edge of social acceptability because of his Native American heritage. His family works hard, becomes wealthy, and sends Julian to Yale so that he has the educational imprimatur of success and respectability. According to William Nelson, he is the "comic reversal of the noble savage" ("Comic Grotesque" 37; "Unlikely Heroes" 165). Bonanza Jellybean differs from others because she has her mysterious scar in her belly and has always wanted to be a cowpoke. Her parents even force her to a child psychologist in an effort to correct Jelly's goal of being a cowgirl. Like Sissy's family, Jelly's parents worry about her freakishness. Jelly's desire is outside of accepted gender roles. Like her nickname "Jelly," Bonanza Jellybean is sandwiched between her desires for a future when girls can choose careers as a real cowpoke and pressure to conform to socially condoned female aspirations (352).

Like Jelly, the Countess also stretches the boundaries of gender identities and lives on the edge of society. He successfully exploits that society, however, and as a consequence enjoys wealth. He is a man who calls himself the Countess. He despises the smell of the female body and has, therefore, made a fortune selling sprays and douches to camouflage the female vaginal odor. He employs Sissy as a model but always hides her thumbs in her photographs. The Countess represents a challenge for Sissy because he enables Sissy's survival while simultaneously endorsing only the acceptable female roles for Sissy. The Countess does tolerate Sissy's hitchhiking, but only because he believes the marriage of Sissy and Julian will make Sissy settle down. The Countess's role as a surrogate parent ends when Sissy erupts with anger at him and beats him with her thumbs, her most valued trait. The Countess has insisted that they be hidden and erased. The Countess's rejection of Sissy because she refuses to conform to the traditional wifely role hurts Sissy's self-esteem, causing doubts in the otherwise confident woman. Ironically Sissy does seek the surgery to "correct" her thumbs after she beats the Countess. Thus Sissy's rebellion, which has led to violence, causes her to seek the very conformity that the Countess has wanted for her. The Countess represents in one person the patriarchal desire for control. Sissy finally rebels against the patriarchy which has been causing her self-doubt and confusion. In her efforts, she becomes violent against the representative of those forces, the Countess. This scenario foreshadows the confrontation at the Rubber Rose Ranch when the rebellious cowgirls engage in armed struggle with the government agencies. Both cases involve rebellion, violent resistance, and restoration to self-acceptance.

Under the direction of Delores Del Ruby, the cowgirls illustrate the same ironic circle of rebelling as Sissy, and then absorption of the very force that they have rebelled against. They use the same tactics as the patriarchal agencies: they hold the beautiful whooping cranes hostage by drugging them so that their natural radar devices fail. The cranes do not know which direction to go, so they stay where they are instead of completing the annual migration. The hands also destroy all of the buildings of the ranch, so that not even the outhouses are left. In their defiance, the cowhands become patriarchal in their control and their violence. Delores poses as a tough, unyielding leader. She finds inspiration in isolating herself in the mountains and taking peyote buttons.

Her consultations with the peyote and the earth mother provide her with visions that direct the actions of the cowhand rebellion. Her final vision directs her to lead the cowhands in peaceful surrender. Delores is formidable; her skills with the whip keep her followers in line. Her challengers and enemies must face the whip as well as Delores's tongue. A gender reversal describes Delores's leadership style. Unlike the patriarchy, she consults intuition instead of logic for her plans, but she behaves like a patriarchal leader in demanding fulfillment of her orders. Eventually intuition wins over her demand for power, and Del Ruby calls for the cowgirls to surrender.

The Japanese-American called the Chink behaves as the opposite of Delores Del Ruby. In the end, he and Del Ruby will have a meeting of the minds, but in the meantime he lives without stimulants to gain insights. He consults his inner self for direction. He demands nothing of followers or others. He adamantly does not want followers and chases them away by rock throwing and other rude gestures. He refuses to make pronouncements about life except in cryptic riddles. The Chink is the wise one despite his protests, because he has the knowledge which enables him not to preach. He knows that the secret of life (which his pilgrims want from him) is an inner wisdom that individuals must discover for themselves. His sense of the individual and the universe owes its origins to the new physics post-Einstein. Robert Nadeau discusses the inclusion of a quantum mechanical vision of the universe that the Chink recognizes from the example of the Clock people, earlier inhabitants of the caves he lives in. The Clock people have a different concept of time, illustrating for the Chink and the reader the arbitrariness of rules that govern humanity. Because of his insights, the Chink is the implanter of a future vision. Sissy gains from him the final understanding that empowers her to stay true to herself rather than warping herself to fit the Countess and Julian's version of her. The Chink leaves Sissy and Delores and rejoins the Clock people.

Dr. Robbins has the credentials of the traditional psychiatrist. He is finishing his training in a medical residency at Dr. Goldman's clinic and has not succumbed yet to the final brainwashing of the psychiatrist. He can still recognize intuition and native wisdom in an individual. Therefore, he realizes that Sissy is not mentally sick; rather she is the healthiest person among the people at the clinic. Her desire for freedom and her acceptance of her thumbs show a self-respect and self-knowledge that deserve nurturance instead of criticism and rejection.

At the end of the novel readers discover that Dr. Robbins's empathy with Sissy is necessary because Robbins is the person who has gathered together the materials for this report about Sissy and the Rubber Rose. Unlike Marx Marvelous, Dr. Robbins does not interact with Sissy as directly as Marx does with Amanda. He is with her in New York during her therapy at the clinic and joins her at the end of the novel. His knowledge of her life continues because he becomes the Countess's doctor/consultant. Consequently he can influence the Countess to be generous with the rebellious cowpokes and their leader, Delores. He provides Sissy and the cowpokes the means to sustain themselves during the aftermath of the rebellion and in the future.

By the revelation of his role as researcher, Dr. Robbins becomes, then, the Interviewer in Chapter 12. This pose situates the reader and Dr. Robbins as the receivers of a narrative inside the narrative. This double audience establishes the readers as closer to the origin of the story than they are when the author tells them the story. It creates the facade of more immediacy.

STYLE

As with any Tom Robbins novel, style is the most important aspect of *Cowgirls*. Robbins employs a traditional omniscient narrator in this book and follows the expected linear plot. He introduces language that blends the formal, the informal, the profane, and the arcane. He is able to create a multiplicity of voices in the narrative through the reporting of events observed by characters, through the inclusion of letters, and through the narrator's reports of conversations. The narrator of course supplies readers with all of these views because he serves as the listener to Sissy's therapy sessions with him. Dr. Robbins, therefore, hears events from Sissy's point of view. He knows the contents of letters because Sissy shares them with him during their therapy meetings in the garden of the clinic. This style of creating the narrator (and consequently the reader) as voyeur grants Robbins the freedom to change language styles, creating even a style for the offstage critic whom the reporter (Dr. Robbins) must hear criticizing his writing efforts (55, 149, 223). The most entertaining of the voices, this critic reinforces the artificiality of the act of writing, which engages in the fantasy that sentences have a life of their own and suggests that language itself is an entity that controls the writer. Robbins empowers sentences with personalities as in the passage that begins, "This sentence is made of lead ... This sentence is made of yak wool ... This sentence has a crush on Norman Mailer. This sentence is a wino and doesn't care who knows it. *Like many italic sentences, this one has Mafia connections. . . .* This sentence may be pregnant, it missed its period" (124–25). Robbins puns around the fantasy of sentences living and breathing, growing more outrageous as he progresses throughout the passage. Coupled with this humor, however, is the very serious issue of stereotypes and prejudices. The novel exposes the tyranny of prejudice, which stifles individual freedom and universal harmony. Beneath the silliness of the sentence that "doesn't *look* Jewish" lurks anti-Semitism. The ludicrous idea that a sentence can "look" anything exposes the same about people; the "looking" anything as a basis for judgment is superficiality and wrong. Language is alive for the narrator.

Sarcasm ends a flow of sentences that refer to the writing process and the writer's task amidst their humor. A sentence searches for "the perfect paragraph," losing its mind in the process. Alluding to the sometimes-arduous task of composing, one sentence is "made from the blood of the poet" (124). This phrase also alludes to the biblical blood of the lamb, suggesting the writer as martyr. Furthermore, Robbins indicates that the author has no pretensions about the greatness of his writing, stating that the "organic" sentence will not "retain a facsimile of freshness like those sentences of Homer, Shakespeare, Goethe et al. which are loaded with preservatives" (125). This comment suggests a lasting greatness of the writers listed as well as an artificiality to their greatness because of "preservatives" such as critics and English teachers. The self-consciousness of the text represents the style of the narrative in general: the language suggests responses and illustrates in its being the philosophy of its author. The flippancy, the fantasy, and the humor of the style disarm the reader from feeling threatened by the philosophy of the themes underlying the text.

THEME

The major theme of *Even Cowgirls Get the Blues* is freedom, particularly for individual idiosyncrasies. The Chink emphasizes that individuals have only themselves as the source of salvation. No one else can save or salve the person. After Sissy has been stationary for nine months in New York, she again takes to the road hitchhiking to her assignment at the Rubber Rose Ranch. Being able to express herself through her hitchhiking "floods" her with "ecstasy." Her domestic confinement with Julian has changed her from a self as "unwavering as a whooping crane" to one with the ambivalence of a "gull" (127). Sissy's health depends on her ability to exercise her freedom of movement. To be restricted in self-expression leads to self-doubt and violence.

Robbins illustrates this idea not only with Sissy Hankshaw's story but also with the cowgirls. The cowgirls assert control over the ranch by destroying it. Their first step, however, onto the road to pariarchal mimicry is the coralling of the whooping cranes, diverting and stopping the birds from their yearly migration pattern. Patriarchy has allowed people to encroach on the population of whooping cranes to such an extent that the cranes neared extinction. In a mistaken belief that they are protecting the cranes from men who will kill them, the cowgirls interfere with the natural migration pattern of the cranes; the birds cannot express their innate drive for migration. This curtailment of their behavior pleases the cowgirls, who are happy with the domestication of these beautiful, wild, endangered birds, forgetting in their drive for power that the birds will suffer from failing to fulfill their natural instinct. The birds' entrapment by the seductive peyote buttons parallels Sissy's seduction by Julian and marriage. The cowgirls endanger the cranes in just the way that domestication of the female human population threatens healthy female growth and self-expression. Sissy's life with Julian perverts her natural self-expression, resulting in a violent use of her thumbs, which heretofore have always been positive tools of movement. Robbins shows that Sissy's inhibitions and the prohibitions against her natural talent as a hitchhiker and free agent violate her positive self-respect and diminish her so much that aggression is her defense. Self-acceptance and freedom are crucial to positive survival on the planet.

The arbitrariness of behavioral standards as well as abstract concepts such as time and space is the other primary theme of *Cowgirls*. The Chink introduces the relativeness of concepts that Western society has accepted without question. The Clock people have taught the Chink and the readers of the novel that time is an arbitrary measure. They base their time on thirteen months rather than twelve; their day is twenty-six hours long. They moved to burrows under the earth in the Sierras after having witnessed the San Francisco earthquake. They live for a time that they call the Eternity of Joy, which will occur when time itself is destroyed (218–19). The people "experiment freely with styles of life instead of styles of death" (221), accepting that another shift in the landmass will destroy the clockworks, the basis for their daily ritual. They embrace this destruction as inevitable and welcome but live focusing on life instead of anticipating death and deadening life the way traditional religions of the West do. Robbins stresses that he embraces the joy of life rather than death. He rejects writers of depression and doom, calling depression an indulgence in *Jitterbug Perfume*. The Clock people are in tune with the movement of the Earth and reject the trappings of "civilization" as an "insanely complex set of symbols that obscures natural processes and encumbers free movement" (222). Robbins illustrates this perception in the rest of the novel. The government agencies and the outlaw cowgirls feuding over control of the whooping cranes, Julian and the psychiatric clinic opposing Sissy's worldview and calling it neurotic or insane, and the Countess deciding Sissy must marry Julian in order to be tamed are all instances of complex symbolic social structures totally removed from the natural and affirmative life. Ultimately individuals must follow their natural rhythms as long as they do not oppress the rights of others.

A theme that is hardly separable from the above two items is the issue of women's rights to pursue their dreams regardless of their gender. Bonanza Jellybean is the cowgirl hero because her dream is that the daughters that follow her generation will grow up assuming the profession of a cowpoke is natural for a female. Bonanza is a liberal feminist who disagrees with Delores Del Ruby's aggressive demands for power. Debbie and many of the other cowpokes regard Del Ruby's letter to the government agencies as filled with the "same hostile sexism" as that they disliked in men (352). The liberal feminists of the ranch want freedom of movement and dreams fulfilled. They do not want to perpetuate the attack upon patriarchal institutions that the radical feminists in Del Ruby's faction appear to want. Del Ruby gains the wisdom to stop her faction's oppressive behavior by consulting via peyote buttons with the mother goddess. Her insights cannot stop the inevitable force of negativity that she and the rebels have launched, however, and devastation by patriarchal forces ensues; like is answered with like. The individual rather than the group must speak its own truth.

Like Bonanza Jellybean's vision of future equality, Sissy's vision of her life focuses on the freedom to pursue her true nature. Sissy's independence as hitchhiker and female defies the expectations for female behavior. Freedom of movement has not been part of the female experience. The safety of travel can be threatened, if not thwarted, by sexual assault. Sissy's strength of character is so great during her hitchhiking heyday that aggressors refrain from assaulting her. She also devises a strategy using her thumbs that deflects rapists' intentions, but Robbins's portrait of Sissy as enjoying molestations by drivers strains the reader's credulity

(21). The book, however, is fantasy, and the ultimate fantasy for females is safe sexual satisfaction and protection from rape in a world that allows women freedom of movement. This freedom remains unavailable to women as long as any men are socialized into thinking that women's sexuality and bodies are at their disposal regardless of the females' wants.

A recurring motif in Robbins's novels, including *Cowgirls*, is the conflict between logic and intuition. Robbins introduces Sissy's dilemma over her love for Julian and her need to hitchhike with a reflective passage about logic. Julian, the unnatural Native American, has learned to conform to the environs of Yale and New York by invoking "logical thought." He endeavors to instruct Sissy in the process of logical analysis. Robbins introduces Sissy's attempt at logical cogitation with the observation that "rational thought" is actually a game that people play on their brains and often on those of others (133). When Delores Del Ruby is explaining why the structure the cowgirls are building for the cranes is round, she declares that "The square is the product of logic and rationality.... It's the work of masculine consciousness.... That's why in civilized societies woman's lot—and Nature's lot—has been such a sorry one" (348). Del Ruby articulates in this incident the basis of Robbins's analysis of gender relations: man is the unnatural, and women need to reorient men to the natural. Del Ruby phrases it as "It's the duty of advanced women to teach men to love the circle again" (348).

ALTERNATE READING: FEMINIST

An intuitive approach to understanding *Even Cowgirls Get the Blues* invites a feminist analysis. Women's reception of this book has been strong but mixed, as some have declared *Cowgirls* a liberating text for females and others have condemned the book as sexist. The book contains considerable ambiguity which at least provokes reflection and analysis. For the sake of simplicity, the positive feminist analysis finishes this chapter.

Feminist literary theories can be loosely categorized by the questions each theory asks of texts about women. The latest generation of the feminist movement that began in the sixties initially considered literary texts according to the images of women they contained. This images-of-women approach to books by men in particular was an important stage in a search for concrete evidence of female stereotyping and for understanding the impact of texts on women's sense of self. The second focus of feminist investigation became one of the recovery of women writers, artists, and historical figures, for numerous creative women ignored or suppressed by the academy and the general sexist culture had been buried. This recovery and analysis work began to answer the crucial question of why there had been no great women artists (Nochlin). Along with these two approaches to texts, feminist theorists began investigating the social, cultural, and economic implications of women's texts. Male texts became less of interest once the images-of-women approach to interpretation seemed to be exhausted. Studying women's texts became the primary focus for feminist analysis. Feminist scholars began reading women writers for their messages about the fate of females. Patricia Meyers Spacks introduced the idea that many female texts before the feminist movement actually contained "subterranean challenges" to the patriarchal expectations of women (317). Rereadings of Jane Austen, George Eliot, Charlotte Brontë, and Emily Brontë highlight this effort at understanding female artists as foremothers. Virginia Woolf became the inspiration for many of these analysts. Her clearly articulated feminism and recognition of women's need to have creative mothers that provide inspiration and courage appealed to countless scholars and students. In her classic text *A Room of One's Own* Woolf declared that "We think back through our mothers" (79). Feminists also apply, among other theories, psychological, Marxist, sociological, and structuralist approaches to texts. An important movement in feminist theory is the French feminists' work on texts. The theoretical investigations of Luce Irigaray focus on language. She interprets texts by males, looking at their use of language, particularly the question of gender distinctions in language usage. Julia Kristeva has critiqued the psychoanalytic approach to the human mind, among other traditional Western philosophical movements. Hélène Cixous investigates from an essentialist point of view the differences between female and male language. She sees biological variations as the reason and need for a female language.

The approach to use with Robbins's *Cowgirls* is the images-of-women theory. The images-of-women approach to analyzing texts delineates a list of common stereotypes that males usually employ when portraying female characters. Male writers tend to depict women as virgins, whores, mothers, or bitches. Within these stereotypes is the seductress, which is part of the whore image. The mother includes the controlling female who infantilizes the male. The bitch castrates men, emasculating and using them for her own purposes. The most common fate for these female characters is death or marriage. The virgin who falls from her pedestal suffers for her sins by dying (Patrick Suskind's *Perfume*; Henry James's *Daisy Miller*). The mother who dares to yearn for more than nurturing children and family must die (Count Leo Tolstoy's *Anna Karenina*). If the characters survive, they live severely hampered lives in physical suffering or enslaved by responsibilities that result from their straying from their expected behavior (Henry James's *Portrait of a Lady*). Unfortunately even though these images became delineated and discussed in scholarly as well as popular publications, many male writers persist in using them. The majority of novels written by males even in the 1990s continues to punish women for their existence. Any deviation from the submissive wife or woman must exact the price of life or maiming or marriage to a restrictive but wiser man. Marriage demands submission to the rule of the male. Often the female character is enthralled by her love and willing to sacrifice or do anything for it. Marriage means that she embraces the role of wife and necessarily mother if she is to be a good woman. The bad woman who feels or exhibits discontent with her wifely role is portayed as deviant, unwomanly, and probably insane. Sissy Hankshaw Gitche embodies the female who triumphs over the forces that try to tame her into submission to the wifely, confined role of the woman. In fact Sissy celebrates female freedom of movement and sexuality.

Although Robbins employs the rebellious-wife motif in *Even Cowgirls Get the Blues*, he creates, however, a new image that defies the repertoire of female stereotypes—the free woman. The free woman in *Cowgirls* allows her natural self-expression, fulfills herself with a creative career, and enjoys her sexuality. Because society still rejects such a woman, she may live this life only on the outskirts of civilization, in the Dakota hills rather than in a town or city. She does live, rather than die, at the end of the book.

The novel opens with the hero Sissy as a patient at Dr. Goldman's mental health clinic. She has refused to settle for the submissive-wife role and now must prove her sanity. By the end of the story, she has left the patriarchal asylum and her marriage for freedom in the Dakota hills.

Robbins's novel depicts the passage of the growing girl through the vicissitudes of life as a female hero. Like many heroes, she momentarily succumbs to a seduction that diverts her from the hero's path. Sissy submits to the traditional female wife role until she reaches the feminist haven of the Rubber Rose and finds alternatives to conformity. The questions aroused by her experience at the Rubber Rose cause her to refuse the Countess's (her boss) and Julian's (her spouse) control over her life. After angrily beating the Countess with her thumbs, Sissy learns that violence simply destroys and hurts rather than solves her problems. Her fear upon discovering the dangerous power her thumbs have when used as weapons seduces her again into denying her thumbs and her hitch-hiking freedom. She undergoes an operation to reduce her thumbs to social normalcy, but as the first thumb is healing, she answers the call of distress at the Rubber Rose. Her remaining oversized thumb enables her to reach the ranch in an attempt to stave off disaster. Her thumb size becomes positive again when she uses it for its natural purpose. Sissy learns to accept her freedom and power, realizing that positive strength results from following the natural rather than deforming the natural for artificial conformity. Sissy reaches freedom as the mother of the future race of humans.

Robbins's portrait of a female with a frank enjoyment of sexuality hall-marks another deviation from the traditional literary image of woman. Sissy's oversized thumbs cause concern for her traditional 1950s family. Her mother particularly worries about Sissy's chances of marrying. When she takes Sissy to a fortune-teller, her questions focus on Sissy's finding a mate. The mother's dreams will be fulfilled not only with approximately five grandchildren but also with multiple mates for Sissy of both genders. The chagrined mother hustles Sissy away from the fortune-teller, even allowing her to hitchhike home, hoping to avoid any embarrassing questions from her daughter. The future sexuality of her daughter surprises Mrs. Hankshaw despite her worry about finding a future mate for her. Marriage is the mother's preoccupation, not sexuality.

Contrary to the usual punishment in literature of women who express their sexuality, Robbins creates a female hero with open curiosity about and enjoyment of her sexuality. Sissy remains virginal despite her molestations at the hands of drivers who give her rides. Her sexual activity, however, is not extensive in relation to the casualness of encounters practiced in the 1960s and 1970s. Her partners are unusual because each is marginalized. Julian Gitche and the Chink represent the unnatural and natural man, respectively. Bonanza Jellybean and Delores Del Ruby represent two extremes of feminism—the liberal, who believes in change from within the current system, and the radical, who believes equality can arrive only through the segregation of male and female. Sissy mates with all of these characters, serving as a bridge between the divisions that these extremes represent. According to the Chink, children born with large thumbs will be unable to operate the tools of war. Sissy is the peacemaker, and Dr. Robbins seems at the end of the novel to be her future collaborator and mate. Therefore, the end of Sissy's quest is pregnancy in the Dakota hills. Rather than a traditional marriage victimization by submission, Sissy's pregnancy is liberation for her and future generations of people. The female hero triumphs as creator of a master race of gentle, peaceful, large-thumbed people.

Rather than girls who play with dolls as they grow up, Robbins describes girls who practice their future professions. Sissy plays hitchhiking games; Bonanza Jellybean prepares for a cowpoke career. As a coming-of-age novel, *Cowgirls* presents the career concerns of girls as primary, with love as a secondary but important goal. The usual image of women as they enter adolescence is as love-struck or love-seeking females searching for their mates. The cowgirls turn to same-sex relationships when no men are available on the ranch. Gratifying their sexual energy rather than finding love serves as their entertainment. Bonanza Jellybean's lifelong goal has been to be a professional cowpoke with serious cattle ranching as her responsibility rather than sideshow exhibitions at rodeos. Just as Sissy runs away from home when her family is about to sign her on as an exhibit in the Colonel's freak show, Bonanza resists her family's efforts to normalize her. She refuses to function as a social freak but aims for her goal as a serious rancher and for a time when little girls can assume that they can be cowgirls if they want to be. Robbins defies the stereotypes of women used in novels about female lives, providing a refreshing alternative to death or a deadly marriage.

Still Life with Woodpecker
(1980)

Tom Robbins's formulation of the premise of a novel usually takes the form of a title or a central event. The germ for Robbins's *Still Life with Woodpecker* was the idea of writing about objects *"for their own sake"* rather than symbolically (McCaffery & Gregory 234). He decided that the mythology and lore of the Camel cigarette package was the most culturally resonant. In fact the Camel packaging has so much lore attributed to it that Robbins knows of many more stories about the Camel pack than those he uses in the novel. The novel resulting from this approach to objecthood became a best-seller. Robbins's book signings were mobbed by fans eager to have him autograph their copies of the book and to talk to their hero.

PLOT DEVELOPMENT

Unlike his first and second books, *Still Life with Woodpecker* follows a fairly straightforward narrative line which unfolds the story of Princess Leigh-Cheri and Bernard Mickey Wrangle, alias The Woodpecker, chronologically. Robbins specifically uses the fairy tale known as "The Frog Prince" (Christy 130). The opening paragraphs of the novel resemble the tone and style of a classic fairy-tale introduction. Further developing the fairy-tale motif are the characters of a princess, her parents, the king and queen, the outlaw, and the servant. As in many fairy tales that contain princesses, Robbins's novel revolves around the love story of Princess Leigh-Cheri and Bernard Mickey Wrangle, both redheads. The princess believes in group action to protect the environment. The Woodpecker disdains groups as deadening to the spirit and mind of the individual. He champions individual action as an anarchist bomber. The couple meets in Hawaii where Leigh-Cheri has gone to attend an environmental conference and to see her hero, Ralph Nader. The Woodpecker has gone to bomb the conference in protest against institutionalizing a political movement. Falling in love despite their opposing views of political action, Leigh-Cheri and Bernard eventually overcome their differences. The love of the princess and her suitor is star-crossed, as love usually is in a fairy tale, and the princess and her lover spend time imprisoned away from each other. Leigh-Cheri realizes that the Woodpecker has a good point about mass movements and group thinking and enacts her own form of protest by constructing a prison for herself in the family attic, remaining there until the Woodpecker is freed from jail for the bombings he has committed. Unfortunately the Princess's self-imposed imprisonment makes the news, and thousands of people follow her example to prove their love. Her individual expression of devotion becomes a group movement despite her new awareness and renunciation of mass action. Leigh-Cheri, stung by Bernard's letter rebuking her for her action, entertains Bernard's competitor for the princess's love. At the command of Leigh-Cheri, the Arabian prince builds a pyramid to prove his desire for her. The star-crossed lovers, however, reunite, are together incarcerated in the pyramid, escape, and end the story living together in middle-class American bliss, unable to hear because of the explosion the princess uses to gain their freedom from the pyramid.

Honoring the influence of things such as the moon on people, Robbins divides the novel into sections labeled by the phases of the moon. The Woodpecker teaches Leigh-Cheri about "lunaception," a method of birth control based on the moon phases and women's menstrual cycles. Since Leigh-Cheri has already had an unfortunate pregnancy when a cheerleader, this information becomes significant to her as a sign of Bernard's consideration for his partner. The moon is also a mythological symbol for the Great Mother Goddess, or moon goddess. In Greek and Roman myth, the moon represents Artemis and Diana, goddesses of the hunt and of virgins. Robbins supplies readers with a list of her various manifestations: "The Moon Goddess, the Great Mother, the feminine principle of creation, growth, change, and renewal. The Moon Goddess is the oldest recorded and most universally common deity ... this Queen of Love, this giver of fantasies and dreams, this Shepherdess of the Stars" (189). Since Leigh-Cheri is a love-struck romantic and Bernard Mickey Wrangle a bomb-laying martial outlaw, the union of these two characters equals a fusion of the two sides of the Great Mother, love and war.

CHARACTERS

Since *Still Life with Woodpecker* has a central theme of how to make love stay, Robbins employs a fairy-tale formula as the basis for the novel. Since love staying is something of a fairy tale in itself, according to cynics, and since love being found and the fairy-tale couple living happily ever after is the basic stuff of fairy tales, Robbins populates his novel with fairy-tale characters. Appropriately this extended fairy tale of a novel contains, besides a king, a queen, and a princess, a faithful old crone retainer, a prince, an outlaw, a chauffeur who is a spy, and a toad.

King Max and Queen Tilli live in political exile in the Puget Sound area of the United States. The CIA provides them with their drafty mansion. They are basically ineffective figureheads who try to adjust to their exile. King Max becomes a gambler. After open heart surgery in which a valve is replaced, he can no longer play poker because the metallic click of the heart valve indicates when he gets excited. He consoles himself by playing poker with the chauffeur and CIA spy, Chuck, and by watching sports. Queen Tilli has gained too much weight from attending society events. She spends her days changing clothes and putting on makeup for her endless cultural events. Her beloved companion is a chihuahua. Both royals spend their time in bewildered waiting that becomes less patient and grateful to the CIA as the years pass. They have abandoned hope of monarchy being restored to their kingdom. Their sons are in Europe making money in dubious business deals. Their remaining child is their daughter, whom they hope to marry advantageously. They indulge their daughter's whims mostly as the easiest way to cope with her.

Their daughter, Princess Leigh-Cheri, becomes a pregnant cheerleader. Her despair over the failure of birth control and over her tarnished image leads her to mature and take herself seriously. She embarks on a conscientious study of world causes, particularly the environment, and joins the movement in preparation for the remote possibility of returning to rule her homeland after its current dictator loses control. Leigh-Cheri

epitomizes the romantic temperament. In reaction to the disappoint-
ments of her teen pregnancy and miscarriage, Leigh-Cheri attempts to
squelch her pursuit of the romantic; "romantic fantasies were . . . *imma-
ture*" she decides (21). Her efforts to concentrate on world problems such
as the environment become sidetracked when she meets fellow redhead
Bernard Mickey Wrangle. She fails to resist romance once more and
makes the ultimate romantic gesture short of suicide, an old-fashioned
concept left for German poets, by creating a prison for herself in the
family attic so that she will experience the deprivations that Bernard will
endure as he serves his prison sentence for his bomb escapades. Leigh-
Cheri acts sincerely in all of her causes, be it cheerleading, solving world
problems, or proving her love. She decides to use her status as a princess
to accomplish good in the world. Her symbolic self-imprisonment enables her to coordinate her body's cycles with the moon. She develops a
different sense of time, following the natural rhythm of the lunar cycle.
Leigh-Cheri resembles in this sense the various cave dwellers and her-
mits who populate Robbins's novels. Princess Leigh-Cheri becomes the
moon goddess during her meditations on that entity and on the symbolism of the Camel cigarette package. Leigh-Cheri's moon contemplations connect the novel's structure with her story. Robbins divides the
novel into the phases of the moon, and Leigh-Cheri's fortunes wax and
wane in accord. Leigh-Cheri's romanticism is a tribute to the Moon Goddess or the Mother Goddess who is also the Queen of Love, according
to the text and mythology (189). The Moon Goddess appears in the symbolism of the Camel pack, thereby connecting the pyramid structure on
the package with Leigh-Cheri's own meditations on the moon. Leigh-
Cheri's romantic imagination convinces her that Bernard must share her
contemplations and interpretations of the Camel pack. Her efforts to re-
strain her romantic fantasies, therefore, prove to be in vain, and Leigh-
Cheri continues to function as the embodiment of the Moon Goddess.

   Leigh-Cheri also represents the modern conflict between the romantic,
or the natural, and the rational, or scientific impulses. The conflict is the
classic struggle within her between the individual and the whole. Her
private self-imprisonment becomes public, and Leigh-Cheri's act of romantic solidarity with Bernard metamorphizes into a mass movement of
copycats. The princess cannot escape her role as romantic icon despite
her efforts. She seems forever doomed to be "dragon bait," as Bernard
pronounces her (98).

   Despite the princess and the outlaw's rejections of it, romanticism wins
in the end. Robbins shows the unity of Bernard and Leigh-Cheri after

their shared escape from the pyramid. Their joint incarceration serves to unite the sensibilities of the two lovers. When in their separate prisons, Leigh-Cheri believes Bernard is having the same thoughts as she. While in the pyramid, she discovers that he did not contemplate the Camel pack as she did. When talking after their escape, they learn that while in the pyramid they shared the same dream precisely down to minute details. Robbins indicates through this common dream that the two of them have reached a shared vision. Leigh-Cheri's definition of true romance is possible after all. They live happily ever after in a blackberry-covered mansion in the Northwest of the United States.

Eighty-some-year-old Gulietta, the faithful retainer of King Max and Queen Tilli and Leigh-Cheri's nurse, becomes queen of King Max's old kingdom. Leigh-Cheri is content to renounce princesshood, having found true love with Bernard. Changing the world no longer serves as Leigh-Cheri's purpose; instead, overthrowing stereotypes and sharing a vision with Bernard satisfy her. In their married life, both of them spend time apart from each other, meditating in their own parts of the house. Leigh-Cheri takes up painting as her avocation. Bernard carries around matches. Deaf from the blast that rescued them from suffocation in their pyramid prison, each has a hearing aid in appropriate male and female colors but cannot hear completely even with the aid. Their sex life is great and continuous. Choice wins the day. The Princess chooses her role in life rather than succumbing to roles pushed on her by society. Leigh-Cheri, then, develops from a romantic social activist and dragon bait to a romantic individual, satisfied with the mystery of love instead of wanting global happiness or the moon.

Bernard Mickey Wrangle represents the outlaw individual as an anarchist bomber. His red hair earns him the name "the Woodpecker" and serves as a primal link between him and Leigh-Cheri. He is staunchly against collective group action, advocating a philosophy of CHOICE, in capitals as Robbins writes it. Groups stifle individual choice and are, therefore, bad. Bernard's definition of an outlaw rests on the distinction between a criminal and an outlaw. The difference between them is that "criminals are frequently victims, outlaws never are. Indeed, the first step toward becoming a true outlaw is the *refusal* to be victimized" (63). People who subject themselves to others' laws are victims. Outlaws are beyond laws; they do not create their own laws, but live "beyond society" (64). In fact Bernard believes that outlaws "raise the exhilaration content of the universe" (64). He appreciates the "self-conscious romanticism of the outlaw" (65) and all of the attendant myths and images such as the outlaw's traditional black clothing. Bernard is a romantic just as Leigh-Cheri is, but he develops a philosophy of the individual, emphasizing individual choice and responsibility. The group hides the inaction of the individual by compensating for the individual who fails to sustain the spirit or action of the group. Likewise the group dictates the individual's action; therefore the group allows the individual to act without responsibility. He or she can make the group responsible for whatever she or he does in the name of the group cause.

The Woodpecker's philosophy dismisses organizations operating as a whole instead of the individual. Not only must people accept responsibility for their own action or inaction, but also each individual must actively choose personal beliefs and courses of action or inaction. The Woodpecker's philosophy is integral to his character since it determines the manner in which he relates to the world and to other people. He requires unique behavior of himself, including the bombing of institutions he deplores as the representatives of groupthink. One could interpret Bernard Mickey Wrangle as a romantic of the opposite extreme of Princess Leigh-Cheri. This shared romanticism links the two lovers as much as their shared red hair color.

Queen Tilli and King Max function as the anti-majesty. Both of them have accepted their exile as rulers with resignation at first. Later as Leigh-Cheri matures, they rejuvenate at the prospect of their daughter as the possible replacement for the repressive regime in their former kingdom, which is now threatened with instability. Their characters embrace the bathos of their new life in the United States, distracting themselves via gambling and sports for the king, and for the queen, through changing clothes and attending ladies' clubs, especially the opera society. Leigh-Cheri's unfortunate pregnancies startle them out of their selfabsorptions long enough for them to allow her to attend the Care Fest conference in Hawaii, chaperoned by the servant Gulietta. Her selfincarceration also interrupts their preoccupations long enough for them to worry about Leigh-Cheri's welfare.

With their renewed sense of purpose, rejuvenated in their own ways, King Max and Queen Tilli are in seemingly good shape. But King Max dies from the excitement of gambling again. Tilli reaches the most congenial position of all in the family by returning to their kingdom and resuming her opera work. She reaches fulfillment with this resolution of her fate. When Gulietta, instead of Leigh-Cheri, becomes the country's monarch, the royal family accepts the event with equanimity. Ruling their country is not their desire; they simply want the status and comfort of being in their own land. Gulietta is welcome to take the responsibility for the fate of the country. The anti-regal behaviors of the king and queen establish that monarchs are simply people with rather common human traits and problems such as not understanding their children and not knowing good parenting skills. The king and queen reject their respective stereotypes. Ruling a country is no fun. They would rather have the wealth and respect granted monarchy without the responsibilities.

The faithful servant Gulietta, the last remaining from the royal household, represents a complex blending of the faithful nursemaid to the princess and an individual who has human drives and weaknesses, such as sex and addiction. At first she appears to epitomize the classic servant; soon, however, Gulietta is revealed to be as much a maverick as her employers. At eighty, Gulietta has the energy to maintain the rambling mansion, cook six meals a day (the princess is a vegetarian), and tend to all the other caretaking needs of the family. Even though she speaks only her native tongue and the princess speaks only English, Gulietta performs the traditional role of storyteller to the child princess. She behaves, however, as if she could transform the fairy-tale myths into reality. She presents Leigh-Cheri with a toad after observing the princess's shame and sadness over her public miscarriage while cheerleading for the University of Washington game. Leigh-Cheri houses the toad, which she ironically calls Prince Charming, at the end of her bed. Gulietta, believing in its special powers, tries to take the toad, along with her new bikini, to Hawaii. When the ruling junta leaves their former kingdom, Leigh-Cheri does not become ruler, but Gulietta takes command. As the representative of the working class, Gulietta serves as a fitting leader for the revolutionary government. Gulietta's story is a fairy tale come true, as is Leigh-Cheri's union and reunion with Bernard "The Woodpecker" Mickey Wrangle. Robbins's reversal of fairy-tale character roles does not negate the myth that fairy tales can come true. Gulietta has become ruler of her country; Leigh-Cheri and her true love live happily ever after, and so in her society sphere does Queen Tilli. Robbins therefore challenges but confirms fairy-tale romance.

Even though she hopes and then demonstrates that fairy tales can come true, Gulietta is not a simple, one-dimensional servant. Robbins gives her human and humane traits. That she cares deeply for Leigh-Cheri is clear from her gift of the toad. She also plays as hard as she works. The eighty-year-old outfits herself with a bikini for Hawaii, celebrating her body and reveling in the beach. While enjoying the sand and surf, she becomes hooked on cocaine after Bernard introduces it to her. The highly addictive crack cocaine was not around in the 1970s, and the less potent but still addictive powdered cocaine remained debated during that time as to its addictive qualities. Executives, stars, lawyers, and other highly paid individuals used powdered cocaine as their drug of choice. The drug situation and knowledge about drugs have changed considerably since the release of *Still Life*. Robbins has since stated that he regrets having shown characters having approved cocaine usage. He does show that because she needs money to buy the expensive drug after the supply from Bernard Mickey Wrangle has run out, Gulietta demands payment for her work for the first time. In a new assertiveness, she institutes a strike, which disturbs King Max and Queen Tilli more perhaps than Leigh-Cheri's self-incarceration in the attic. Gulietta continues to help Leigh-Cheri but carries her picket sign with her when she runs the Princess's errands. The rebellion of Gulietta prepares readers for her eventual assumption of the leadership of their homeland. Her energy and spirit make her political role logical. She treats Max and Tilli fairly, providing them with enough money to live in dignified independence from the United States. She also extends her concern to Leigh-Cheri despite the princess's move to her fiancé's distant Arabian country. Gulietta travels to be with Leigh-Cheri for her wedding to A'ben Fizel and shares her supply of cocaine with the princess. As a monarch, Gulietta takes control of the country instead of rubber-stamping the programs of the rebels. One of her policies makes the country a nuclear-free zone. Gulietta proves that an over eighty-year-old woman and the working-class population can retain vitality, intelligence, and joie de vivre. Humor surrounds this turn of events as well, because no one expects a person such as Gulietta, a cocaine user, to be the ruler of a country and sensitive to environmental issues. Robbins reverses the expectations that many people would have about a character such as Gulietta. The nurturing ruler–old crone Gulietta, who contains some of the old fairy-tale traits, illustrates the positive implications of female rule.

The Remington SL3 typewriter fills no role in fairy tales, but it does serve as a character in this book. It does parallel the tradition of authors who claim that a power other than themselves actually wrote a text. In a sense Robbins parodies writers such as Harriet Beecher Stowe who asserted that God directed her writing, filling pages with words through the use of her body and pen. The ultimate relinquishing of responsibility occurs in such cases. Robbins undermines Bernard's philosophy of CHOICE when he uses the Remington SL3 as a character. The SL3 itself types rebellious and irreverent comments about the narrative, its characters, and its narrator. When it refuses to submit to the discipline of typing the narrator's words, the narrator takes over the text, and writes by hand the end of the epilogue. The SL3 anticipates the comments of critics; plays devil's advocate in philosophical discussions about the moon, love, and life; and reminds readers that they are having a wonderful time reading a narrative rather than watching or hearing one.

STYLE

Still Life with Woodpecker opens with a prologue personifying a typewriter as the cocreator of the text. Immediately Robbins thrusts the reader into the consciousness of the creative act as a construction. The typewriter, a Remington SL3, contains the "novel of my dreams" (prologue). Somehow the typewriter is more than the recorder of the author's words; it is a creative force of its own freed by the writer's fingers. The fantasy of the machine as capable of creating also introduces the idea of the object as an entity unto itself rather than as a symbol. Robbins describes this phenomenon with sentences such as: "This baby speaks electric Shakespeare at the slightest provocation and will rap out a page and a half if you just look at it hard" (ix). Making a joke about his old Olivetti typewriter, Robbins compares juggling and writing, reminding the reader of the creativity and construction involved in novel writing: "There is, however, a similarity between juggling and composing on the typewriter. The trick is, when you spill something, make it look like part of the act" (ix). Robbins, however, makes readers aware of the act itself rather than pretending that the act of writing is seamless reality. As "Interludes" and interjections anywhere in the text, comments about the typewriter and the creative process interrupt the otherwise direct plot line of the novel.[1] Robbins ends the novel with a handwritten epilogue because the typewriter has "gotten out of hand" in its ramblings. Besides adding humor to the text, this alienation technique is more realistic than the pretense that the novel is reality. It presents the creative act as it is: a process of interaction between the writer's mind, the instruments of writing, the page of paper, and the reader.

Robbins includes much language play in the forms of puns, neologisms, nonce words, and repeated lines in *Still Life with Woodpecker*. He punctuates Queen Tilli's speeches with the refrain "Oh-Oh, spaghetti-o." The other refrain throughout the novel is "Redheads burn easily." These repeated lines serve much as punch lines in a comic's routine. Their banality and predictability create the humor. Incongruity also plays a role in the humor of Queen Tilli's "Oh-Oh" since a queen is expected to speak in a refined manner and not quote television commercials. In another method of creating humor, Robbins employs figurative language that defies convention; he creates analogies and similes based on highly original combinations of images. In one such case, Robbins describes Leigh-Cheri's reaction when asked about her nonexistent love life by comparing her teardrops to "bronco amoebae leaving the chutes in a biology lab rodeo" (76). The surprise of comparing tears to rodeo horses causes the reader to pause to consider the image and laugh at it. On consideration, the analogy fits perfectly as a description of someone crying in jerky sobs.

THEMES

In an interview with Tom Robbins, Sinda Gregory lists two issues that she sees in *Still Life*: "romantic love and outlawism" (McCaffery & Gregory 233). Robbins responds to her statement by adding to that list "objecthood." Gregory summarizes these themes by asserting that Robbins imbues them with a facet of spirituality. These four themes will form the basis for the analysis of this novel.

Spirituality suffuses the novel because all of the characters and objects struggle with understanding its essence. According to Robbins's books spirituality comes from within the individual without the need of any outside force or organization to instruct the person in proper spirituality or the way to be spiritual. The tyranny of organized religion and its killing of spirituality simply by becoming an institution occur as a theme in Robbins's first novel, *Another Roadside Attraction*, and to a less obvious degree in *Even Cowgirls Get the Blues*. *Still Life with Woodpecker* emphasizes the individual and objects as spiritual entities. The moon and a typewriter have soul; people recognizing this truth lead fuller lives. They pursue their spiritual potential as individuals and recognize that potential in all creatures and creations. A respect for spirituality includes resisting attempts to organize or dictate to others their method of expressing or pursuing spirituality. Therefore, organized religions kill spirituality. Movements that start from theories which champion spirituality but then become politicized and organized lose the essence of their original spirituality. Robbins uses the women's movement as an example of such an event (see "Feminismo" and *Cowgirls*). In *Still Life* Robbins uses the environmentalist Care

Fest as an example of a good cause that goes awry because mass organization removes the individual action and spirituality from the heart of environmental preservation. One man—Ralph Nader—becomes the leader of the movement, diluting the possibility of individual initiative through reliance on a leader. Changing a spiritual or social goal into a unified group following one leader, whether he or she consciously pursues that role or not, removes from participants the sense of individual autonomy, creativity, and responsibility in favor of a group mentality. This group-think destroys true spirituality.

Juxtaposed to spirituality in humans as a major theme in *Still Life* is the state of objecthood, though Robbins expands this theme far more in his fifth novel, *Skinny Legs and All*. In *Still Life* objects stop short of becoming animate characters, although the lace on a pair of Leigh-Cheri's underpants does squeal when Bernard unknowingly steps on it while exiting a taxi (106).

The primary object contemplated in *Still Life* is the Camel cigarette package. Leigh-Cheri takes a pack with her into her makeshift prison attic because Bernard smokes this brand. As she meditates on the significance of the pyramid, the camel, and other iconography on the package, Leigh-Cheri believes that she is spiritually closer to and, therefore, communicating with Bernard. Instead of the camel speaking with her or in any other way communicating with her, the camel receives Leigh-Cheri's imposed interpretation. Leigh-Cheri projects feelings and thoughts onto the camel and imagines it galloping across the desert. She imposes meaning on the pyramid, the eye, and the trees as well. Robbins interjects the thought that people interact with objects and this interaction then has impact on the human and the object. Humans, however, fail to acknowledge this symbiotic relationship and dismiss any spiritual nature or reciprocity with objects. Reading a book, the narrator observes, is a function of the sort of interaction between human and object that Robbins postulates. The narrator declares that the reader, no matter how willing or unwilling, has a relationship with a text, just as Leigh-Cheri has one with the Camel pack and the moon (169). A common object-human link is the lunar cycle correlation with the female menstrual cycle. Although it is not scientifically accurate, Robbins has Leigh-Cheri synchronize her female hormonal cycle with the moon's monthly traverse. Bernard teaches her this lunaception as a means of birth control. Through her contemplation of inanimates, Leigh-Cheri is cured of her "animate chauvinism," as the narrator calls her indifference to the sensibility of objects (220).

Robbins elucidates the human-object connection with three other major "inanimates"—the moon, the pyramid, and the typewriter. The moon and the pyramid function as both public and private signifiers. If conditions allow, all people who care to look into the night sky can see the moon, as can all people in the vicinity of a pyramid see it. These objects, then, function publicly with perpetual availability to viewers, given the restraints of time of day, season, weather, and place. Simultaneously as these objects function publicly, they operate as private symbols or signifiers for each viewer. The human regarding the object assigns his or her own meaning to the object; therefore, lovers describe "their moon" and observers assign their interpretation to the presence of a pyramid. Robbins's narrator delineates these distinctions in the following manner: "The moon is about as public as a thing can be. Yet the moon seldom fails to invoke a sense of intimacy" (238). The narrator in this passage is arguing against a hypothetical dean of inanimate objects at Outlaw College. The narrator maintains that humans assign significance to objects because objects do have influence on humans, as illustrated by the moon's "light and gravitational pull" (238).

The argument between the narrator and the dean of inanimate objects ends because of the third "inanimate object" to possess a major presence throughout the novel. Just discussing the typewriter as a character establishes the soul and spirit of the object. But the SL3 is much more than a character. The Remington SL3 typewriter, in fact, is presented as the actual creator of this narrative. It is fused to the narrator so that the narrator uses the first-person plural "we" during discussions of the Remington SL3's mood, opinion, and health. The public/private argument over the moon and the pyramid ends with the following report about the typewriter: "The Remington SL3 is running on empty, and what with thousands of people . . . pouring in for the pyramid unveiling and the grandest wedding of the decade, we have more than we can handle right now" (239). Robbins's narrator embodies the fusion or influence of object and human with a self-presentation that slips from the third-person reference to the typewriter into the first-person plural, which unconsciously for the narrator—not for Robbins—reveals the influence of the object on the human. The narrator and typewriter are one, suggesting that objectivity (the state of being an object), being (as in human), and creativity are inseparable. Perhaps the poet W. B. Yeats's conundrum serves best to illustrate the point: how does one tell the dancer from the dance?

The Remington SL3 is so important to the narrative that it is the catalyst for the novel's first and last words, cast as a prologue and epilogue.

In case readers become too enamored with the philosophical implications of Robbins's speculations about objects, he has the narrator take control of the narrative by handwriting the last few pages and ridiculing as pseudophilosophical the novel's discussions about objects, life, and the individual. He ends the book with a popular banal slogan about childhood and happiness as if to undercut any efforts to attach serious meaning to the text. Readers, however, will be influenced by the book, as Robbins has had the narrator already assert. So despite efforts by Robbins and his narrator to forestall any philosophical musings suggested by the text, the reader will assign his or her own significance to the narrator's and the Remington's words. In further challenge to interpreters of the book, Robbins has the Remington spouting the themes of the novel that readers would identify. This passage in the epilogue not only suggests the power of the objective (the typewriter) but also the pervasiveness of the subjective (the reader's view). Once again Robbins fuses the public and private, illustrating that the acts of reading and comprehending are simultaneously public and private. The subjective and objective merge to suggest that these categories are purely arbitrary themselves.

Robbins's exposé of the arbitrariness of categories such as objective and subjective, private and public, illustrates that neither are as mutually exclusive as Western philosophy claims. A feminist reading of this text would suggest that Robbins employs the revolutionary feminist perspective "the personal is political" throughout *Still Life with Woodpecker*. In Toril Moi's book on sexual and textual issues feminist critics Elaine Showalter and Patricia Stubbs argue that a truthful picture of women "would include equal emphasis on the private and the public" (7). Robbins's main characters, Princess Leigh-Cheri, Bernard Woody Wrangle, and the servant, Gulietta, embody the individual history as well as the public conception of a princess, an outlaw, and a faithful old crone. Although the book contains the basic formula of the fairy tale with its archetypically named characters, its king, queen, and princess, and its rambling old bramble-encrusted mansion substituting for a castle, the plot of the book reverses the usual prince-rescuing-the princess motif. This reversal makes an images approach essential to an understanding of the novel. An Anglo-American reading of this text would look at the images of women and their treatment in the book. Literary critics such as Kate Millett, Mary Ellmann, and Mary Ann Ferguson pioneered the feminist analysis of male writers' treatment of women in literature. Although feminist theories have grown to encompass more sophisticated,

postmodern approaches to textual analysis, this 1970s interpretation harmonizes with the social commentary contained in Robbins's *Still Life with
Woodpecker*. Reading Robbins's manipulation of fairy-tale figures with a
feminist perspective also coincides with the rewriting of fairy tales that
many feminists have accomplished.[2]

The three primary female characters of the book—the princess, Leigh-
Cheri; the queen, Tilli; and the servant, Gulietta—are figures common in
literature and myth. Ordinarily this triangle of females becomes embroiled in a curse or a contest for the hand of the princess in marriage.
The queen represents either evil, as in a wicked stepmother (think Cin-
derella), or a nonentity as in a hand-wringing ineffective bystander in
the drama of her daughter's fate (think of the story of Snow White or
Shakespeare's Juliet). The queens, therefore, are either malevolent or
powerless. Queen Tilli seems benign if distant from her daughter. Princess Leigh-Cheri's dramatic disasters—her teen pregnancy, her public
miscarriage, her self-incarceration in the attic—attract the queen's attention and, consequently, the king's. She does want to be a good enough
mother, although it is not her primary role. Her major concern about
Leigh-Cheri is that the princess will ruin her chances for an advanta-
geous marriage. Later in the novel Leigh-Cheri becomes valuable to her
parents because rebels in their homeland consider Leigh-Cheri a potential new ruler for the country. The sons in the family are unfit because
of dubious financial dealings and connections. Despite her princesshood,
Leigh-Cheri is not interested in the role of monarch. After fulfilling the
traditional American princess and female ideal of cheerleader and failing
that ideal by becoming pregnant, Leigh-Cheri considers herself ready to
be an adult and, to demonstrate that, feels responsible for the world's
improvement. Environmental causes attract her energy. Ralph Nader becomes her ecological guru.

Social consciousness is not usually associated with being a princess.
The princess archetype involves falling under a curse that can only be
broken by a worthy prince. The princess must wait for the right prince
to come along. Sometimes toads test a princess's kindness by pleading
for her kiss to turn them back into princes. As faithful, nurturing attendant, Gulietta gives Leigh-Cheri the toad she names Prince Charming
and whom she does occasionally kiss just in case he really is a prince
underneath the amphibious skin. In its own interesting twist of this motif, *Beauty and the Beast* employs this test motif as well in that the girl's
trust and kindness can change an animal into a princely man.

The outlaw Bernard Mickey Wrangle appears and liberates the princess from the spell of Ralph Nader and mass movements. In this incident Bernard plays the traditional prince awakening the princess from a spell. He also liberates her from the celibacy she has adopted because of the tyranny of nature's hormonal cycles leading to pregnancy. Resisting the hero role, he declares that his intention was not to rescue Leigh-Cheri as though she were dragon bait (99).

Bernard is an anarchist and, therefore, not the royal family's ideal as an acceptable suitor for their daughter. Most of the princes in fairy tales are proving their suitability to belong to the royal kingdom's society and to marry the princess. Bernard, however, is not interested in establishing his propriety as a son-in-law. His quest is not proving himself capable as a hero. He rejects the cultish worship of one person. He acts alone as an anarchist, having lost his gang of merry followers like Robin Hood. He embraces the lore and stereotypes of the outlaw, distinguishing between outlaw and criminal activity. The outlaw is beyond the law; the criminal is a victim (63–64). His purpose in Hawaii focuses on bombing and disrupting the massive Care Fest. Princess Leigh-Cheri is an incidental diversion that sidetracks Bernard's bombing plans. His attraction to her becomes a desire to divest himself of his bombing past and be with her.

The couple discuss their relative roles as social and mythological icons early in their relationship. The princess represents "Enchantment, dramatic prophesies, swans swimming in castle moats, dragon bait" (97) and "fairy-tale balls and dragon bait" (98). Unlike the fairy-tale hero who rescues the princess from a fire-breathing dragon who keeps her prisoner, the outlaw figure wears black clothing and represents "uncertainty, insecurity, surprise, disorder, unlawfulness, bad taste, fun, and things that go boom in the night" (98). The outlaw does; the princess waits. Bernard enjoys his role as outlaw, but Princess Leigh-Cheri flatly rejects the passive "dragon bait" prescription for females of her rank. Leigh-Cheri declares that she is "as capable of rescuing" Bernard as he is of rescuing her. Similarly Bernard claims that he "never intended" to rescue Leigh-Cheri and play the prince. He thinks that people must rescue themselves from their own dragons because every human being creates her or his own interior dragons (99).

By the end of the novel Bernard and Princess Leigh-Cheri have traded roles. He remains an outlaw, running from his imprisonment, but he is under the magic spell of romanticism. After Gulietta persuades the

United States to release Bernard from prison, Bernard travels to A'ben Fizel's kingdom to bomb the top off the pyramid Fizel has built to honor Leigh-Cheri's request.

The roles of bomber and dragon bait reverse in the pyramid while Bernard and Leigh-Cheri are imprisoned. Bernard believes that igniting his dynamite will kill them rather than blast them free. Leigh-Cheri reaches the decision to use the dynamite regardless of its threat since their lives are almost over from lack of food and water. Bernard believes her intention is to sacrifice her life to save his and reflects on "the princess as hero" (263). When they reunite in the hospital after the explosion, Leigh-Cheri writes "Hello, dragon bait" in greeting Bernard (266), thereby completing the role reversal of the two characters.

Contrary to most fairy-tale practice, which ends the story with the marriage of the happy royal couple, Robbins continues the love story into their lives as married people. The princess and the bomber create a middle-class life. They watch the television, copulate, and pursue their own hobbies. In another switch of traditional male and female gender roles, Robbins gives Leigh-Cheri the active hobby of painting and Bernard the less productive pastime of carrying around wooden matches in honor of his former bombing life. Both are deaf from the bomb blast in the pyramid and therefore communicate better perhaps than many hearing couples who fail to listen to what the other is actually saying. Leigh-Cheri then ends as a painting princess with a happy sex and married life instead of leading her kingdom. Since the major theme of Bernard's outlaw life has been CHOICE, Robbins indicates with Leigh-Cheri that choice of one's life is more important than fulfilling society's ideas of one's role. Neither the traditional passive princess waiting to be rescued nor the role reversal of feminist ruling monarch interests Leigh-Cheri. She chooses a quiet life with her equal partner. Robbins affirms in their relationship that the choice of individuals weighs more as an influence on the world than mass movements. The equality of Leigh-Cheri and Bernard enables them to live happily.

Robbins, however, does not abandon the chance of creating a strong female character. Gulietta develops from the stereotypical faithful old servant to the royal family (and Leigh-Cheri in particular) into a benevolent, socially conscious ruler of her country. Robbins plays with several conventions of fairy tales and romance novels in the figure of Gulietta. She is the last of a dying breed of servants who remain faithful to their masters through prosperity and reversal of fortune. She believes in magical powers even though she cannot practice them. Her language remains that of the mother tongue of her homeland. Leigh-Cheri knows nothing of that language, but the two of them communicate well. Every night Gulietta tells Leigh-Cheri a bedtime story in their homeland's language, and the princess understands the essence of the tale. Gulietta also supplies a toad for the princess, believing it might have some magic power. Prince Charming, the toad, becomes a totem for the two women, and Gulietta is distraught that officials refuse her permission to take him along to Hawaii. Leigh-Cheri tells Bernard the bedtime story that Gulietta tells her (134–40). In it a princess promises a toad that she will let it live with her if it retrieves her golden ball, which has fallen into deep water beyond her reach. The princess tries to renege on her promises, but her father, the king, demands that she keep her promises. After flinging the frog across the room, the princess discovers a prince released from the frog body. Leigh-Cheri ponders the implications of a prince who reveals his true identity after such rough treatment rather than after the usual kiss. Bernard ponders the fate of the golden ball. Robbins invokes for readers the entire fairy-tale tradition by recreating such a tale in the middle of his narrative. The novel and the fairy tale are both fantasy, he implies, but both have the same moral; that is, individuals must honor their promises and responsibilities.

A plastic frog filled with cocaine replaces Gulietta's customary living toad as her favorite companion after Bernard introduces her and the princess to the charms of cocaine. This frog possesses magic no living amphibian can supply, although certain frogs are known to supply hallucinogens to people in other hemispheres. With the introduction of the trip to Hawaii for Leigh-Cheri and Gulietta, Robbins registers the first aberration in Gulietta's portrait as the stereotypical faithful old crone. On hearing that she will accompany the princess to the Care Fest, the octogenarian Gulietta procures herself a bikini. She has no qualms about enjoying her body despite society's prohibitions against older people being sensual or sexual. Her role as guardian also does not inhibit Gulietta's human love for pleasure. The introduction of drugs into Gulietta's perspective overthrows another stereotype about the straightlaced and uptight nature of most older people. Gulietta's snorting flouts convention and establishes further her refusal to be limited by society's concept of age- and gender-appropriate behavior.

Gulietta subverts another aspect of her stereotype as faithful retainer later in the narrative by going on strike against the king and queen's economic and labor exploitation of her as she realizes the need for more money to supply herself with cocaine. She rejects the passivity of her role because the drug dependency creates needs that she has never had before. In her devotion to Leigh-Cheri, however, Gulietta remains steadfast, continuing to care for the princess even while on strike.

Rejecting her position of subservience to the royal couple does not mean an entire loss of nurturing feeling or responsibility for Gulietta. This trait prepares readers for the changes that Gulietta institutes after she becomes ruler of the kingdom of Mu. In another use of fairy-tale convention, Robbins has the rebels in the Furstenberg-Barcalona homeland discover papers that prove Gulietta is the sister of King Max. The secret identity or long-lost relative is a motif common in myth and romance. Gulietta has known her relationship to Max all along but kept it quiet to stay with Leigh-Cheri. Now the rebels want her to lead the country, and she is ready to comply with their request. She has broken the spell of servitude and grown to take responsibility for who she is. Gulietta epitomizes the positive results of female power by creating policies that are peaceful, ecologically sane, and humane. She does not punish her brother for his stinginess but enables him and his queen to live comfortably with dignity and independence from the government of the United States. She uses her power to gain the freeedom of Bernard so that Leigh-Cheri and her love may be united. Nuclear materials may not enter the country, coinciding with the nuclear-free zone policies that countries such as New Zealand have adopted.

Gulietta, then, is a fairy-tale godmother with more on her mind than ball dresses and Prince Charmings for her princess charge. The most liberating portrait of the entire novel is this one of the eighty-year-old woman establishing a benign rule over a country and maintaining a human link and concern for her earlier responsibility, Leigh-Cheri. Gulietta respects other people rather than neglecting them once she gains power. A feminist reading of her character would interpret Gulietta as a positive and empowering example of woman at her best. The traditionally labeled female trait of nurturing becomes the ideal method for ruling the world, but individual responsibility for one's actions and one's needs remain constants in this world. Enabling Gulietta to serve as a model ruler is her transformation from a stereotype into a self-respecting individual. She realizes that she deserves better treatment and more respect from her employers and begins demanding that she receive improved work conditions. This woman respects herself and enjoys herself as well as her body. Interestingly, the rebels first select her for their leader not only because she represents the traditional monarchy, but also because she is of the people, having served her life as peasant house-keeper to the monarchy. She represents the hero worker as leader to the rebels. They fail, however, to reckon with her new self-respect, not anticipating her efforts to lead the country and institute policies. The rebels' stereotype of Gulietta fails just as much as the faithful old servant stereotype. In the end Gulietta, the people, and women are triumphant.

This application of the images-of-women interpretation to *Still Life with Woodpecker* is just one feminist method of approaching Robbins's portraits of females. Other feminist readings could criticize Robbins for having Leigh-Cheri choose love and domestic bliss over an active role using her powers as princess. Gulietta's cocaine-snorting habit undercuts her seriousness as a role model, and her bikini wearing could be viewed as a comedic attempt at absurdity by using the incongruity of an eighty-year-old woman wearing a bathing suit more commonly associated with a much younger woman. The idea of an older woman as a sexual being or object can be used as a belittling humorous portrait. Readers need to remember that although Robbins interjects humor throughout his books, underlying philosophies are serious to him. He distinguishes between important humor and unimportant humor in an interview with Larry McCaffery and Sinda Gregory. Important humor, as in *Still Life*, presses into the "inappropriate area of humor" and becomes then revelatory and liberating (232). The questionable taste of Gulietta's portrayal pushes the boundaries of appropriate humor and reveals to readers their stereotypes about aging women. Humor is the essence of survival amidst the chaos, despair, and exigencies of life; depressing self-absorption denies the value of life and human creativity. Therefore, the humor in Robbins's portraits of characters should not deny the serious implications underlying their portrayal.

A feminist interpretation of *Still Life with Woodpecker* can also read this text as promoting a key concept of liberation politics: choice. The ability to choose creates an equality among characters and a spiritual freedom. The question of how to make love stay receives several attempts at answers from the narrator, Leigh-Cheri, and Bernard. The action of the text, however, provides the clearest possible resolution to this conundrum; before love can stay, both lovers must be equal. Leigh-Cheri and Bernard's relationship practices hero and princess status for both of the love partners; it is not just a matter of each acting according to their assigned gender and mythic role. Because of this balancing between the interdependent roles of princess and hero, the male and female are complex individuals sharing life and their responsibilities. A feminist definition of ideal gender relationships involves the equality of the people within an interdependent partnership.

Still Life with Woodpecker opens for exploration political and social issues that continue to perplex humans. It also resonates with certain of the late twentieth-century preoccupations that Robbins's next book, *Jitterbug Perfume*, will show to be mythic in their persistence over centuries of human inquiry.

NOTES

1. Robbins actually did paint his typewriter one day in exasperation just as the narrator indicates in the interlude on page 123. See also McCaffery and Gregory on these interruptions to the text as comments that remind the reader that reading is a unique experience that is fun (230).

2. For some feminist rewritings of fairy tales and myths, see Anne Sexton, *Transformations*; Olga Broumas, *Beginning with 'O'*; Margaret Atwood, *Good Bones and Simple Murders*; Angela Carter, *The Bloody Chamber*, and the Attic Press series, *Fairytales for Feminists*.

Jitterbug Perfume
(1984)

Continuing to express his fascination with objecthood, Tom Robbins initiates *Jitterbug Perfume*'s lively series of picaresque adventures with a meditation upon the beet. As readers soon discover, the novel's events are structured around the various quests of its several significant characters—all of whom in one way or another, consciously or not, are interested in the secret contained within that "most intense of vegetables," that "melancholy" (1) plant, the common beet. Among the assorted virtues that Robbins celebrates within his poetic paean to the beet is this passing thought: If there is no blood to be squeezed from the turnip, the same can never be said of the reassuringly ruddy beet. With this observation and a catalogue of others, Robbins claims a place, as one witty reviewer would have it, within the literary tradition of the "beet poets" (Dougherty 124).[1] In the scheme of *Jitterbug Perfume*'s elaborate plot, the beet is an enigmatic presence, regularly appearing and then reappearing in the lives of all the characters. The beet, this novel drolly suggests, is an object worthy of contemplation.

Writing about *Jitterbug Perfume*, novelist Rudy Rucker remarks, "It would be hard to find any other book that even mentions beets, yet this intricate book, about perfume and immortality, has beets on nearly every page. Why?" (9). The answer lies in Robbins's penchant for inviting readers to contemplate the surprising ways in which everything can sometimes be perceived to be connected. In his fourth book it is the beet that serves the poet-novelist as a locus of connections, on one hand linking the centuries-old histories of one set of characters with the contemporary pursuits of another set and on the other hand providing a striking emblem for the whimsical theory of "floral consciousness" with which the novel plays. Robbins is undeniably fond of spinning speculative theories about evolutionary stages of perception and experience.[2] Mixing myth with tidbits of scientific knowledge, he envisions in *Jitterbug Perfume*'s delightful vegetable mysticism the form that a new stage of human consciousness might take.

PLOT DEVELOPMENT

While Tom Robbins himself has frequently stated that neither plotting nor characterization is as central to his interests as crafting the vibrant sentence, as attempting "to weave a tapestry" (Edlin 42) with language, *Jitterbug Perfume*'s plot is masterfully constructed. Indeed, critics have particularly remarked on the ingenuity of plot development in this novel: writing a review for the *Washington Post*, Rudy Rucker finds the "book . . . lovingly plotted, with every conceivable loose end nailed down tight" (9), and the *San Francisco Chronicle*'s Peter Delacorte notes that "everything comes together very nicely; every last thread of an extremely intricate plot is properly sewn together" (1). Given the fact that the plot traverses at least ten different settings (including a visit to the afterlife), hopscotches across a thousand years of history, and incorporates accounts of the experiences of no fewer than seven major characters, Robbins's achievement is not slight.

Readers are introduced to three of its central characters early in the novel. Priscilla Partido, Seattle's "genius waitress"; Madame Devalier, "Queen of the Good Smells" within the French Quarter of New Orleans; and Marcel LeFever, owner of Paris's most sensitive nose, are all the recipients of unexplained and anonymous gifts of beets. Because each of these three figures is intent upon finding the special ingredient needed to perfect an extraordinary jasmine scent, the question arises, as indeed it occurs to Marcel LeFever, "What is the message a beet bears to a perfumer? This beet . . . is it a warning or friendly advice?" (65). To answer LeFever's question, another tale need be told, and thus readers are transported by means of an enthralling flashback to an earlier era, a time when two lovers' pursuit of immortality inspires the discovery of a magnificent perfume. In joining together the interlocking elements of his plot,

Robbins fabricates, as Peter Delacorte observes, "an amalgam of just about every narrative form known to the human race" (1). Through a story that mixes myth with history and folklore with literary allusion, the world is shown to be a place of many wonders.

At the heart of *Jitterbug Perfume*'s plot is the romance of Alobar and Kudra, characters who have lived full lives long before they ever become lovers and who, after they have linked their destinies together, manage to make love stay for centuries. Alobar's story, that of a medieval Bohemian king condemned by custom to die when signs of aging hint that his virility will fade, begins in the tenth century. Ruler of a small tribe whose vegetable staple is the beet, King Alobar is husband to many wives and mighty warrior to a people who have grown fierce upon their regular diet of beets. Neighboring kingdoms have begun to embrace a new religion, called Christianity, but in King Alobar's domain the old traditions still prevail. Thus, when white hairs appear during the king's thirty-seventh year, Noog, the village necromancer, sets a date for execution.

No coward, but rather a hero who has risked his life in many a battle, King Alobar is nevertheless unwilling to die, to take his place among the "time-trapped kings" (23) who have gone before him. He is, as he says, "seized with desire to be something *more*. Something whose echo can drown out the rattle of death" (24). With the assistance of his favorite wife, Wren, he survives his ritual sacrifice, abandons his ancestral home, and takes up the journey that will lead to his quest for immortality. In defying the natural customs of his land and positioning himself outside its laws, Alobar joins Plucky Purcell, Sissy Hankshaw, The Woodpecker, and others of Robbins's characters who stubbornly refuse to be victimized by the societies in which they dwell. Suffering shame but no remorse, Alobar affirms the as yet untested possibilities of life in purposefully choosing to evade death.

If the deposed ruler has hoped that relinquishing his crown will afford him opportunity to quietly live out the natural course of his years, he soon discovers that social condemnation can be the lot of the serf as readily as that of the king. Having taken up residence in Aelfric, a nearby community where turnips rather than beets are consumed, Alobar dutifully attends Christian services and enjoys a peaceful family life among the local peasants. Whereas it was a hair that brought about his first undoing, in Aelfric it turns out to be a bean. Beneath the veneer of their Christian faith, the serfs maintain practice of their traditional pagan customs. Christmas Day opens a festival that celebrates the King of the Bean.

The male who discovers a bean in his cake rules the carnival for twelve days, and then, on Epiphany, the throat of the "king" is cut. Alobar, now twice marked the sacrificial victim, is forced to conclude that he does "not like the way death does business" (41) and therefore resolves to set forth on a quest to discover if it is possible to permanently elude it.

Part I of the novel, entitled "The Hair and the Bean," closes when Alobar, with inspired exuberance, begins the second leg of his journey. Having learned from Aelfric's shaman that "the world is round round round" (45) and having decided that "existence can be rearranged" (45), the heroic adventurer, like Gilgamesh[3] before him, is ready to travel to exotic lands in search of the secrets of the immortals. Leaving behind the dismal city-states of Central Europe, all beginning to crumble under the onslaught of the Christian Romans, Alobar heads to the southeast, making his way toward India. It is at this point in his narrative that Robbins introduces the road novel motif (see discussion in chapter 4) as well as elements of the fabulist tradition (passing through Greece, for example, Alobar meets the Great God Pan, *Jitterbug Perfume*'s most odoriferous character). Thus, as its hero's purpose changes direction, the novel's tone shifts in mood; with Alobar's decision to take to the road, the dark spell cast by the curses of the hair and the bean is abruptly lifted. Alobar has chosen the lot of the outlaw (see chapter 5).

Because Alobar is an outlaw, a refugee from the social penalty of the death sentence, it is altogether fitting that the great love of his life is an outlaw too. In India Alobar meets Kudra, the woman who introduces him to the sensual pleasures of fragrance and kissing (in tenth-century Europe, kissing was unknown; Alobar's people affectionately rubbed noses). Alobar first encounters Kudra when, as a horrified child of eight, she has just witnessed the gruesome spectacle of the ritual of suttee. The older man tries to comfort the weeping child by suggesting that she eat the beets that she is carrying, but in India "the beet is rarely eaten because its color is suggestive of blood" (76). When Alobar and Kudra meet a second time, twenty years have passed, and Kudra, now a widow herself, has abandoned her children and fled her village to escape the flames of her husband's funeral pyre. Like Alobar, Kudra refuses the role of victim.

Jitterbug Perfume is both a road novel and an account of a mythic quest. Because both of these plot motifs traditionally invite an episodic narrative style, the novel can generally be seen as a recounting of the various adventures of characters who seek a goal. All of the major characters,

Alobar and Kudra, Priscilla Partido, Madame Devalier, Marcel LeFever, Pan, and Wiggs Dannyboy (a flamboyant figure who makes a late entry in the story) are intent upon making discoveries that could change the course of their lives. As is often the case, however, in quest adventures, several of these seekers end up finding something other (or more) than the sought-after goal.

In keeping with the road novel motif, Alobar and Kudra experience many wonderful adventures during their centuries of travel. After leaving the Tibetan lamasery where they have become reacquainted, they cross dangerous passes in the foothills of Chomolungma (known today as Mt. Everest). Lingering in the deserted caves of the mysterious Bandaloop doctors, they acquire the disciplines needed to prevent their bodies from aging. After a sojourn in Constantinople and a trip to Greece to visit Pan, the couple spends the Middle Ages wandering the breadth of Europe. There they survive "wars, robbers, fires, pillages, plagues (including the Black Death of 1347–1350), and the intolerances of the Church" as well as "freezing winters, famines, Gothic art, and uncomfortable furniture" (155). Always forced to move along (when neighbors grow suspicious of them), the two eventually join a wandering band of Logipciens, or Gypsies. When even the Gypsies turn against them and they must once again make their way alone, Kudra grows weary of their peregrinations. Pointing out that their long lives have become "selfish and covert and none too easy" (160), she expresses her desire to finally settle down.

Although their quest for immortality has largely been successful (Pan earlier did warn Alobar that "immortality has its limits" [147]) and although the couple has beyond all question remained in love, Kudra comes to feel that something more is now required. If Freud was wise when he asserted that people need both love and work, then Kudra's restlessness reflects that very piece of wisdom: it is the sense of purpose that can be satisfied by an occupation that is absent from their lives. Alobar, of course, experienced that sense of purpose long ago when he was king, but Kudra's ambitions have remained unfulfilled. Born to a caste of incense makers, she longs to take up her family's traditional profession. Kudra and Alobar therefore decide to open an incense shop in Paris; because Louis XIV's court is unacquainted with the refreshing practice of bathing, they believe that they can find there a ready market for their wares.

Much like the beets that reappear throughout the course of the novel, *Jitterbug Perfume*'s characters keep turning up anew. It is while they are establishing their incense business that Alobar and Kudra once again hear news of Pan. The gods, it seems, are only immortal as long as people can care about them. Once faith in them dies, the gods simply fade. Because interest in Pan has greatly diminished during the Christian era, he has in fact become invisible, existing now as only a voice and a stench. Determined to rescue their old friend, Alobar and Kudra conceive a magnificent new plan. Their lives are charged with purpose when they decide to accompany Pan to the New World. There they will "establish a new Arkadia" and indeed "found a race of immortals, with Pan as their principal deity" (166). To succeed in their endeavor, they need first to create a perfume that can "obscure the bouquet of rutting goat" (168) and, second, to earn the fare for their Atlantic voyage.

Jitterbug Perfume's plot takes another marvelous turn when the lovers' objectives become difficult to realize. Kudra does locate two ingredients of the perfume she seeks, but her combination of jasmine and citron requires yet another element, a strong base note that can seal the mixture's scent. The missing element proves elusive, and the couple's savings are exhausted in the course of their search. They therefore decide to approach their problem from a new and radical angle: if they can dematerialize their bodies and then rematerialize in the New World, they can avoid the expense of the journey by ship. This experiment is successful, but just as Alobar begins to spiral free of his material form, he realizes that essence of beet pollen is precisely the ingredient needed to perfect Kudra's elegant perfume. Hastily returning, therefore, to his physical state of being, he finds that Kudra is gone.

Although its flashback sequence occupies a significant portion of the novel, Robbins never lets readers forget that his contemporary characters are searching for the very secrets that Alobar and Kudra have long since uncovered. While Priscilla Partido, Madame Devalier, and Marcel LeFever all aspire to replicate K23, Alobar's hauntingly beautiful perfume, Wiggs Dannyboy, organizer and patron of the Last Laugh Foundation, industriously explores the possibility of achieving immortality. Therefore, at the end of each installment of the lovers' continuing adventures, the narrator conscientiously brings readers up to date on developments in Seattle, New Orleans, and Paris. Hence *Jitterbug Perfume* is composed of an intricate complex of stories within stories. Just as the flashback is a story within the broader account of the other characters' quests, their independent stories are all parts of the whole of the tale. In the end, when each character realizes her or his ultimate goal, all of the stories are linked.

As details of the questers' stories gradually emerge, Robbins carefully weaves unexpected connections among these disparate characters into the fabric of his plot. Alobar, as it happens, is destined to cross paths with the other major characters, and this occurs years after he and Pan have indeed sailed to the New World (K23 successfully masks Pan's "caprine" aroma, but the hapless god becomes severely disoriented when he can no longer smell his familiar old funk). Alobar, of course, had earlier waited for Kudra to rematerialize, but when this did not happen, he resumed his efforts to rescue Pan. His goal, since the day of Kudra's disappearance, has been to somehow find his lover again. Perhaps, he thinks, he too will eventually dematerialize, but in the meantime he runs a spa in rural Montana, serves as a custodian in Albert Einstein's office, and creates a small uproar by bombing MIT's genetics lab. It is this latter event that leads to his acquaintance with Wiggs Dannyboy (and through him to the group of perfumers), for Wiggs and "Al Barr" spend time together as cellmates in Concord State Prison.

It is only fitting, in a story where the beet has played a significant role, that *Jitterbug Perfume*'s characters pay homage to the vegetable that has figured so curiously in all their lives. Thus, as the novel nears its denouement, and its characters approach the end of their quests, readers are treated to the spectacle of a veritable parade of giant beets. Attending the Mardi Gras festivities in New Orleans, Alobar, Priscilla, and Marcel sport exceptionally handsome red and green beet costumes. Gazing through the eyeholes in their stems, the beets (appropriately enough) watch for the approach of the float dedicated to celebration of none other than the Great God Pan. Vestiges of a pagan spirit are still to be found, it seems, in the revels of Christendom.

When Wiggs Dannyboy once announced to Priscilla Partido that "unhappiness is the ultimate form o' self-indulgence" (210), he in fact gave voice to one of the novel's central themes. In their various quests, *Jitterbug Perfume*'s characters have aspired to achieve happiness, but they have not always understood where it might lie—or had the wisdom and courage to seek it out. The story's conclusion, therefore, brings to each character revelation of the source of her or his own happiness. Overjoyed at the prospect of presenting their exquisite fragrance to the rest of the world, the perfumers cheerfully agree to collaborate completely in its production. (They decide, too, to name it *Kudra*.) As for Alobar, who now knows that his happiness lies with Kudra, the time is ripe for a new adventure: wanting "to leave this plane where Kudra had left it" (317) so many years before, he plans to dematerialize in Paris. What Alobar and Marcel do not know, as they travel together to Paris, is that it is, at long last, Kudra herself who awaits them there.

CHARACTERS

As figures in quest of a goal, *Jitterbug Perfume*'s major characters are best defined by their aspirations—and, in the end, by the choices that their chances at happiness require them to make. Some of the characters must learn, as Alobar early discovered, that "existence can be rearranged." Priscilla Partido is an excellent case in point. A young divorcée who has been generally disappointed at her lot in life, Pris attempts to concoct the perfect perfume, a goal that arises from her admitted desire to enjoy being rich. (Being rich, she supposes, will somehow make up for the losses of her father and husband.)

Pris sometimes thinks of her goal as a quest for "the perfect taco," and in conceiving of it in this unusual way, she repeats the last words uttered by her dying father. The offspring of a brief Mardi Gras romance, Priscilla never actually knew her mother. Her father, an itinerant preacher and confidence man, left her in the care of Madame Devalier when she was but a baby. Visiting once every year at Mardi Gras time, the Reverend Wally Lester (known to many as Wallet Lifter) deceived his daughter by encouraging her to believe that he was an important businessman, owner of lucrative gold mines. When Madame Devalier finally told Priscilla the truth, she immediately ran off, at age sixteen, to marry Effecto Partido, Argentinian accordion player.

Priscilla's story reveals that what she really wants—but does not acknowledge—is to love someone and to be fully and honestly loved in return. Having felt twice betrayed when her father quite suddenly died, she left Effecto shortly thereafter, determined to seek a fortune in riches in lieu of a fortune in love. Living in Seattle and working as a waitress, Pris spends her off-duty hours tinkering with test tubes and potions. She possesses a blue bottle that contains the last drops of Alobar's K23 (the bottle washed ashore in New Orleans after the frenzied Pan had hurled it into the sea), but she is unable to identify all the ingredients in the perfume. Hoping to receive one of its stipends so that she can focus completely on her goal, Pris joins the Daughters of the Daily Special,[4] an organization dedicated to helping its members realize their creative inclinations.

That Pris is truly looking for love becomes fully apparent when, after

Wiggs Dannyboy has invited her to dine at the Last Laugh Foundation, she quickly finds herself thoroughly smitten with him. (Priscilla, it is clear, has a father fixation: Wiggs is twice her age and Effecto, too, was more than twenty years her senior.) The romance appears to be developing nicely, however, until events conspire to interrupt its course. A bomb blast at the Last Laugh Foundation seriously injures Huxley Anne, Wiggs's only and much beloved daughter. Eventually, Pris is forced to recognize that Wiggs's loyalties will always lie first with his precious child (a cruel irony for Priscilla, so greatly neglected by her own undependable father). Of course, she still has her surrogate quest, but as if the woes of Pris's love life were somehow not enough, she also encounters additional obstacles in her pursuit of that endeavor: already disappointed when she learns that she has not been chosen to receive a stipend, she is further dismayed when she discovers that Alobar's bottle has been stolen from its hiding place. (It is this occurrence that necessitates her trip to New Orleans to search the bottle out.)

Despite her many troubles, Priscilla proves to be a resilient young woman, a person indeed capable of overcoming an urge in indulge in misery. Her life, she realizes, has undeniably presented her with certain "harsh realities" (278), but she has learned from Wiggs that harsh realities are by no means necessarily the only ones. It is, she believes, sometimes possible to "choose which reality one wished to live" (278). She therefore joins ranks with the other perfumers, effects a reconciliation with Madame Devalier, and when it presents itself, seizes her chance at happiness. As it transpires, this opportunity is made manifest in a most unusual fashion. Watching a television documentary, Pris learns about a new dance craze that has recently swept through Argentina. Called the bandaloop, the dance is thought to offer its enthusiasts increased longevity and vigor. One of its proponents, a Señor Partido, has become a millionaire with his popular bandaloop club. When Pris hears that the nightclub is called Priscilla and that its owner has named it after "zee only woman I ever love" (331), she knows what her next destination will be.

Madame Devalier and Marcel LeFever are the other characters who have dedicated themselves to a quest for the perfect perfume. Professional fragrance makers, these two students of the olfactory arts are busily practicing their delicate craft and, at the same time, pursuing their private objectives. Madame Devalier's personal stake in achieving her goal is readily apparent: her shop has fallen on hard times, and, quite simply, she hopes to restore it to its former glory. Working with her assistant, V'lu Jackson, Lily Devalier is intent upon developing a scent that makes use of a rare jasmine that she has acquired from Bingo Pajama, a Jamaican flower peddler who wears a swarm of bees about his head. Lily knows that the top note of her perfume will be tangerine, but she needs a strong base note, one, as she puts it, " 'with a floor of iron' " (62). As readers come to realize, Lily is in fact retracing the steps once taken by Kudra and Alobar. (V'lu Jackson seems to recognize the significance of Alobar's bottle to Lily's quest, for it is she who steals it from Priscilla's apartment.)

The exceedingly stout Madame Lily (she delights in her city's broad range of cuisines) is a thoroughly good-hearted woman. Forced to eke out a living on her sales of love potions and magical "hurricane drops," she aspires to excel once again in her true profession—and, in so doing, to see to the welfare of Priscilla and V'lu. With Alobar's help, these immediate goals are assured, and her fondest hopes finally come to fruition when the other perfumers agree that *Kudra* will bear the label Parfumerie Devalier. Her happiness thus made complete, Madame Lily blubbers with joy.

As for Marcel LeFever, his particular interest in floral scents derives from the personal campaign he is waging to restore the integrity of the perfumer's art. A purist, the owner of the sensitive nose is intensely devoted to rich aromas and therefore disdainful of all deodorants, the nasty and artificial products of petrochemicals. Tired of the "assertive, unisexual, urbane, unromantic, nonmysterious . . . and wholly synthetic" (69) fragrances fashionable in yuppie circles, Marcel believes that the future of perfumery lies in the use of raw materials. A man who contributes generously to environmental causes, Marcel likes to wear a whale mask while sitting in his office. Appreciative, perhaps, of the role that ambergris once played in the history of perfume, Marcel often dons his mask when he desires to contemplate his business. Indeed, Marcel is exceptionally thoughtful about the nature of his calling; he has devised an elaborate theory wherein he speculates that it was in fact the appearance of the fragrant flower that led to the extinction of the dinosaur. Observing further that humankind's large brain provides stupendous storage space for memory and that smell is the sense most closely connected to memory, Marcel concludes that the ancients were right to believe that the "soul receives its sustenance via the sense of smell" (228).

It is serendipitous, given his commitment to a natural fragrance, that Marcel is present when Alobar spills the "beets," as it were, and divulges the formula for K23. Exclaiming "le parfum magnifique!" (313) when he first catches a whiff of the perfect perfume, Marcel knows in that moment the extraordinary happiness that only the most devoted perfumer can know. Satisfied that his part in the *Kudra* enterprise will be to distribute the scent around the world, he is ready to stake one further claim to his happiness. In addition to thinking about perfume when wearing his whale mask, Marcel has thought a great deal about V'lu Jackson. His joy is therefore made complete (and Freud's dictum regarding work and love answered) when V'lu agrees to be his wife.

Although considerably shorter than Alobar's, Dr. Wiggs Dannyboy's history (fashioned after that of Timothy Leary), has also been filled with adventures and quests. Born in Dublin, Wiggs studied anthropology and then accepted an appointment at Harvard. There he experimented with mind-altering drugs, lost his job, and thereafter continued, in one way or another, to focus on raising his consciousness. Imprisoned on a trumped-up marijuana charge, he used his jail time to explore an interest in immortality. (While in prison he also lost an eye and succeeded in impregnating his wife by arranging for his semen to be smuggled out in a dinner roll.)

Inspired by his conversations with Alobar, Wiggs decides, when he is finally released from prison, to pursue in earnest his study of immortality. He therefore moves to Seattle with Huxley Anne and sets up his new foundation. His investigations quickly turn up promising approaches to the problem at hand: Wiggs is intrigued, for example, by a particularly invigorating dance, and he is fascinated by Marcel LeFever's notion that odor, memory, and longevity are all related to one another. Knowing that the beet figured somehow in Alobar's creation of K23, Wiggs acts as facilitator, secretly supplying the perfumers with the vegetable they are not aware they seek.

His many other preoccupations notwithstanding, it is finally his daughter who interests Wiggs most—and it is thus in her destiny that his happiness lies. Like Priscilla and Marcel, Wiggs must seize his opportunity for joy when it unexpectedly presents itself. In his case, that chance occurs when a swarm of bees lights upon Huxley Anne's head. Although the injuries she suffered in the bombing did not, as was feared, turn his daughter into a vegetable, they did leave her obsessed with the vegetable kingdom, most fully at home in the garden or greenhouse. It is therefore a happy moment for Wiggs when the bees that once encircled Bingo Pajama (the swarm terrorized New Orleans after the Jamaican was gunned down in the streets) find their new home at Huxley Anne's brow.

Understanding the ring of bees to be a halo, the emblem of a holy person, Wiggs sees in the bees' gesture confirmation of his theory that a "floral consciousness" will characterize the next stage of human evolution. Bingo Pajama, he believes, was the "prototype of the floral man" (326). When his own Huxley Anne inherits the swarm, Wiggs knows that she, the new queen of the bees, is truly a flower child.

A symbolic spirit[5] as well as an actual character, Pan grows increasingly ethereal over the course of the novel. Immortality, as he once observed, does prove to have its "limits" (147). (Having lost his voice but not his musk, he roams the Wild West with the disintegrated spirit of Coyote, another immortal trickster.) Because he is a god, the quest for happiness that preoccupies the human characters is totally irrelevant to him. Pan is Pan—or, as it is aptly remarked (when Pan attends René Descartes's funeral): "I stink, therefore I am" (134). In Wiggs Dannyboy's cosmology, the ribald goat-god represents the mammalian consciousness that supplanted the reptilian consciousness embodied by the dinosaurs. Pan, then, belongs to a passing era; anticipating the dawn of a new age of consciousness, Wiggs declares that "there is little place for Pan's great stink amidst the perfumed illumination of the flowers" (326). Ironically, the god's destiny (like that of the dinosaurs) is not his own to choose. Nevertheless, as long as memory of Pan remains alive, his stench continues to signal his presence.

While Pan is clearly an example of the archetypal figures who frequently appear in Robbins's fiction, the same can be said for Kudra and Alobar. Questers on a mythic scale, these characters' magnificent journey through time affirms that "a life in progress" is indeed "a thing to behold" (37). Alobar is the traditional hero, the man who perseveres, the outlaw who tries the limits. In his perseverance the hero repeatedly attests to the singular joy of being alive—but, as Pan wisely predicted, even this joy contains its own limit. Thus Alobar finally reaches that limit when he can no longer contemplate life without Kudra. In Kudra readers will readily recognize another of Robbins's incarnations of the earth goddess figure. Kudra represents both the "crazy wisdom" (265) and the transcendent power (she literally transcends her earthly existence) of the feminine life force. Kudra (or Kudra and Wren, for they are both aspects of the goddess of love) transforms Alobar's quest for immortality into a quest for love.

Jitterbug Perfume offers readers the intimate, storytelling voice of an omniscient narrator who delights in well-timed turns of plot and relishes verbal play (in particular, the pun). This narrator, unlike those of *Another Roadside Attraction* or *Even Cowgirls Get the Blues*, takes no active role in the novel's plot. That is not to say, however, that the narrator's voice is indistinct: on the contrary, the storyteller's strong authorial presence is one of the outstanding features of the book. In addition to recounting, foreshadowing, and interpreting events, the narrator embellishes the telling of the tale with numerous asides, amusing observations, and assorted bits of wisdom.

For the most part, *Jitterbug Perfume*'s events are related from a third-person point of view. In other words, the voice is annunciatory in its unfolding of the details of the action. From time to time, however, the narrator directly addresses the reader or engages the reader in the act of narration by using the pronoun "we." As writer, Tom Robbins uses narrative strategies such as these to a couple of different ends. On the one hand, when his narrator directly engages the reader, the effect is that of establishing intimacy between the two. The reader is, in an immediate way, implicated in the fictional world she or he beholds. On the other hand, however, the authorial intrusion can serve another kind of purpose. As noted in previous chapters, Robbins often draws his readers' attention to the fact that a work of fiction is always a construct, a crafted artifact. That the narrative voice can also be used to demonstrate this is readily apparent when, for example, *Jitterbug Perfume*'s narrator interrupts the English text to inform readers that Marcel LeFever is actually speaking in French. A "simultaneous" translation, the narrator goes on to explain, is being transmitted to readers "via literary satellite" (11). A witty ploy, this self-conscious assertion of the magical powers of fiction functions to remind the speaker's audience that the storyteller's art is indeed purposefully shaped from contrivance.

While each of *Jitterbug Perfume*'s multiple plot lines is engrossing in itself, it is in the manner of the stories' telling that they are conjoined to form a saga. Mixing elements of the satiric with an essentially comic vision, the narrative voice provides the idiosyncratic flavor of the novel's attitude and style. In extravagant similes or hyperboles and in Whitmanesque catalogues that tease the tongue, the narrator zestfully sports with the language that embodies the action. Because so much of that action is ultimately dependent upon the beet (otherwise known as the mangel-wurzel), a great deal of the narrator's linguistic fun is likewise directed toward that omnipresent object. Is it with the beet in mind that the narrator so often insists on the alliterative *b*: "[she was] up to her *b*ouffant in the *b*ackwater of *b*oof *b*iz" (62)? Ambergris, the narrator at one point informs the reader, can be derisively known as "*b*ehemoth *b*arf" (170).

STYLE

By the time his fourth book was published, Tom Robbins's reputation as stylist was already attracting a readership delighted with the stream of "can-you-top-this sentences" (Egan, *New York Times* 9) that has become the writer's hallmark. *Jitterbug Perfume* fully answers the expectations of those readers who have developed a taste for Robbins's linguistic playfulness or artistry: some of the novel's extraordinary similes are boisterously imaginative, others beguilingly poetic. In this novel, much of that which is poetic serves Robbins's desire to use language that can invoke sensory apprehension. While the style of the passages devoted to the whale mask and the beet costumes conjures strong visual images, the sensory experience that commands the most attention is the sense of smell.

Jitterbug Perfume is a book designed to excite the nose. From Pan's reeking presence to the olfactory delights promised by K23, a world of odors permeates the world created by the text. Beginning with a description of Priscilla's apartment, where the chemical smell that "greets" her bounds like a "cooped-up pooch" (4), Robbins searches out an idiom that can convey what the experience of smell is all about. Finding themselves invited to attend to nuances of odor, readers themselves can vicariously partake of the many smells that inhabit the novel: the perfumes and deodorants, the distinctive beet pollen, even the rains of Seattle and the foods of New Orleans (Paris, too, offers characteristic aromas, particularly during the reign of Louis XIV). Robbins's genius for blending the poetic with the comic provides a language wherein he can appear to bring his smells to life.

A somewhat subtler stylistic detail in *Jitterbug Perfume* features Robbins's pointed use of allusion to invoke literary contexts beyond the novel. There is, for example, a passing and playful reference to John Irving's *World According to Garp* (277), and Alobar's Wren appears to be a literary salute to Thomas Pynchon's Victoria Wren, a character in *V*. The most telling allusion, however, is the one that calls to mind *Remembrance of Things Past*, Marcel Proust's monumental work. Like the Proustian character named Marcel, Robbins's own Marcel LeFever is a figure obsessed by the relationship between memory and smell.

THEME

One of the inherent qualities of the quest adventure (wherein characters confront obstacles and learn lessons) is that its episodic narrative structure provides ample space for a writer to address a variety of ideas or themes. Using the opportunities provided by his plotting strategies to full advantage, Robbins explores several distinct issues in his novel. His characters, after all, occupy different stations in life and are engaged in separate quests.

As mentioned earlier, *Jitterbug Perfume*'s characters do share a common ground in their desire to achieve happiness. Accordingly, the novel raises interesting questions about the nature of happiness and where it can be found. While all the characters who seek happiness learn lessons about love (Priscilla, for example, learns that wealth cannot answer the absence of her father), Robbins's depiction of Kudra and Marcel also emphasizes the value of satisfying work. Significantly, however, work alone does not lead to happiness. Marcel's ferociously ambitious Uncle Luc expires miserably—collapsing into his ashtray—and Alobar, who works far too hard at simply staying alive, receives a pointed message from the great beyond. Inscribed in Wren's handwriting, the message reads *Erleichda* (ancient Bohemian for *lighten up*). Of course, "lighten up" is one of the recurrent themes in Robbins's fiction. It is therefore not surprising that "Erleichda" turns out to be Albert Einstein's final word.

Besides taking up love, work, happiness, and the message implicit in "Erleichda," Robbins's novel addresses the environmental issues that Marcel LeFever cares about, exposes the superficiality of Luc LeFever's mercenary imagination, and plays with the unusual theories of evolutionary development espoused by Marcel and Wiggs Dannyboy. During their long lives Alobar and Kudra witness numerous examples of the intolerance or injustice practiced by religions or other social institutions, and thus these issues too are among the many themes of interest in the book.

Certainly one of its most intriguing themes, *Jitterbug Perfume*'s Proustian note resonates throughout the novel. Marcel claims that "memories associated with scent are invariably more immediate and more vivid" (228) than those evoked by the other senses. Indeed, his assertion is demonstrated in odd but dramatic fashion when his cousin Claude fails to notice that his father has died and slumped into his ashtray. Claude is oblivious to Luc's fate simply because the odor of smoldering flesh has transported him back to the "distant summer evening" (230) when he and his new bride walked through the clouds of grilled mutton smoke that wafted across Algerian beaches. In this scene and others, characters experience the power of aroma to stir memory, but it is in the book's portrayal of the afterlife (modeled on Egyptian myth) that the relationship between odor and immortalist longings is finally revealed.

When Kudra transcends her material existence, she visits the realm of the dead. Although there is no odor in the huge terminal where the dead line up to learn their ultimate destinations, the entrance plaza is an "ocean of scent" (339). Wren is present, and she explains that the dead arrive swathed in the most cherished aromas from their lives. However, because odor evokes memories that connect the dead to life (thereby promising the hope of an eternal material existence), those who pass through death's portals must relinquish their sense of smell. Odor arouses the mortal being's craving for immortality.

It is, perhaps, in its studies of art and creative endeavor that the novel's most compelling themes are found. The work of art, as exemplified in an elegant perfume, is shown to be a thing both carefully wrought and intricate. Like other works of art, *Kudra* consists of parts; through elaborate processes of distillation and extraction, the perfume's distinct themes must be brought together to create the effect of the whole. While jasmine is *Kudra's* essential substance, this element is not sufficient in itself. An introductory "top note" is required, as well as the solid "bottom note" that can hold the parts together. If it strikes the reader that the art of perfumery is not unlike the art of the novel, then Robbins's text can be seen as self-referential, as an example of the literary work that reflects or comments upon its own artful nature.

In addition to describing the elements of the finished work of art, Robbins's novel depicts the process of creation. Most interestingly, *Jitterbug Perfume* repeatedly offers a model of creative enterprise that flourishes through acts of collaboration. Robbins's conception of the Daughters of the Daily Special provides a good example of the way the idea works: all waitresses, the members of the organization pay steep dues and contribute efforts to fund-raising events so that one of them can use her sabbatical time to create a work of art. Of course, the Daughters are not the only characters committed to artistic enterprise. The perfume called *Kudra* is the most extraordinary work of art created in the novel, and its production also depends upon the collaboration of people whose purposes are diverse. As it happens, the principle of cooperative endeavor can also be applied to the story of Alobar's life. For Alobar, the living of a life is itself an artful undertaking, but one that finally requires the collaboration of his lover. Thus it is Kudra who can provide the "bottom note" that Alobar needs to hold his life together.

ALTERNATE READING: A MARXIST PERSPECTIVE

Marxist criticism, like feminist and cultural criticism, provides a sociological approach to analysis of literature and its cultural context. Broadly speaking, Marxists pose questions about common social practices and about the assumptions that lie behind the ways institutions are organized. A political philosopher who himself witnessed the burgeoning of nineteenth-century industrial society, Karl Marx (1818–73) framed his own questions around the interrelationships he saw among economics, politics, and social classes. Marx's questioning eventually led to a critique of industrial society's inequitable distribution of power and resources and to a theory of history that concentrated upon struggles between the classes. Concerned in particular about the power of the wealthy to exploit the working class, Marx saw that workers who lack the means to enjoy the products of their labors are denied opportunity to share in the true value of their work.

To Marxists, whose theories are based upon a materialist conception of reality, work is essential in human experience. Human societies are always productive, producing the means of their own sustenance as well as the many artifacts that satisfy other needs. (Besides assuring the bare necessities, people's productivity gives expression to the human need to participate in life's purposes or pleasures.) Because it is through its labors that a society's productivity is achieved, work is crucial to its welfare. Nevertheless, when some of those who labor cannot fully partake of the fruits of their own productivity, then their work is devalued. Used by their societies but not counted among those whose contributions are meaningful, such workers cannot enjoy the intrinsic purpose in what they do. When they are deprived of the satisfaction of a sense of purpose, members of the working class often experience estrangement or alienation from the very society that realizes the benefits of their efforts.

While contemporary Marxists continue to expose the deleterious effects of class distinctions, they have also focused their attention upon the ways in which race and gender operate as categories through which people are denied full, free, and valued participation in social life. Because conditions of race, class, or gender can in fact shape a person's opportunities, the concept of ideology is extremely important to Marxist thought. One of the reasons that people remain enmeshed in the confining conditions of their lives is that they are caught up in a system of beliefs and values that forcefully dictates the nature of their expectations. As a Marxist critique of the power of authority generally reveals, it takes a rebellious mind and a brave spirit to call into question the very realities by which societies define themselves.

Early in its pages, *Jitterbug Perfume* offers exceptionally fine illustrations of both the power of ideology and of the kind of divergent thinking that is required to question or challenge it. Alobar and his people belong to a clan knit together by a sense of collective destiny wherein the lot of the individual has no special value. The reason the king must die when his prowess begins to decline is that the people believe that the decay of the leader signals the decay of the tribe. Thus the sacrifice of its king ensures the prosperity, strength, and continuity of the collective society.

Naturally Alobar too subscribes to the beliefs of his people. He knows what his destiny is, and when he finds himself resisting it, he must in good conscience ask himself why. The explanations that occur to him all arise out of the ideology that has defined what his role should be: is he a madman, he wonders, or perhaps a coward? Is his unwillingness to die an act of blasphemy or an exercise of monstrous vanity? Wren, with whom the king discusses his dilemma, cannot understand his puzzling impulse, but she knows that he is neither a madman nor a coward. What Alobar is, of course, is an outlaw. Although he acknowledges to Wren that he is part of "the community, the race, and the species," he is yet "somehow separate from them" (24), and that sense of separation ignites the spark of rebellion that positions him to question the assumptions that have hitherto shaped his life.

Interestingly, Alobar upholds his responsibility to a society that assumes that he must die before it can continue to thrive. In faking his ritual execution, the king allows his people to maintain their confidence in the beliefs that govern their lives. Under their new ruler, the people persist in eating their beets, going to war, and thinking that their world is flat. They go on, that is, as long as they can—the Holy Roman Empire, of course, has no interest in honoring their way of life. The shame that Alobar once felt over his decision to abandon all that he knew to be true is ultimately tempered by the wisdom of the ages. Looking back, after he has outlived the ephemeral history of his kingdom, he sees with the clarity of his perspective that the beliefs of his youth were all illusion.

Kudra's experience is similar to Alobar's, for she resists an ideology that insists a loving wife's place is with her husband. Because her failure to perform her "duty" violates her cherished values, Kudra spends years worrying that she is doomed to be reincarnated as a spider, flea, or worm (violating one's principles does not mean that one has abjured them—such is the power of belief). As Kudra herself observes, the life of the outlaw is not easy: it is a difficult thing to forswear community connections, to live without sharing the purposes, visions, or values of others. Perhaps it is because they are tired of being outsiders that Kudra and Alobar look forward to the new life they envision with Pan.

While the rebellious path of the outlaw offers a way to escape socially prescribed roles, Robbins describes an alternative option in *Jitterbug Perfume*. When people work together, they too can hope to discover ways whereby "existence can be rearranged." The members of the Daughters of the Daily Special clearly lead constricted lives. All women, and members of the working class (despite their college educations), the Daughters lack the time and means to explore their creative inclinations. Although these women live with the daily drudgery of their lot, they all long to produce a truly satisfying piece of work. When they decide to band together, they find that they are able—even if it is only symbolically for some of them—to break free of the confines of their class and gender. The path of the outlaw is a solitary one, but the collaborative project is firmly rooted in the spirit of community.

NOTES

1. The pun is one that Robbins himself would likely appreciate. The concluding section of *Jitterbug Perfume*, entitled "The Bill" and dedicated to poet Darrell Bob Houston, itself summarizes the lesson of the beet in the form of a final pun.

2. Note, for example, the theory of amphibian consciousness elaborated in *Half Asleep in Frog Pajamas* or the lunar/solar dichotomy explored in *Still Life with Woodpecker*. (That novel, as well, offers readers an exotic account of the mysterious history of redheads.)

3. Alobar's pursuit of immortality assumes a place in a long literary tradition of such quests. In the world's earliest epic, the hero Gilgamesh also attempts to learn the secrets of eternal life.

4. Ellen Cherry Charles, waitress, artist, and protagonist of *Skinny Legs and All*, is also a member of the Daughters of the Daily Special. She and Priscilla become acquainted at the group's meetings.

5. There are references to Pan or Pan's odor in others of Robbins's novels. In *Even Cowgirls Get the Blues*, for example, the Chink discourses on the goat-god's

role in the lives of pre-Christian peoples—when Pan was also known as Krishna. Always a seductive figure, the god of fields and flocks embodies the experience of sensual pleasures. In alluding to Pan's musky aroma, Robbins calls attention to the horned god's bawdy nature.

Skinny Legs and All
(1990)

Tom Robbins is not best known as a writer of political novels, but in truth his fiction frequently addresses significant social or political issues. As the early novels demonstrate, Robbins gleefully chooses satire as the prod with which he can excite some of society's sacred cows. In particular, he is interested in critiquing those monolithic institutions that seem to him to stifle individuality or, worse, to incite people to despise one another. As readers of *Another Roadside Attraction* well remember, organized religion ranks high on his list of these kinds of institutions. It is not altogether surprising, then, that in his most overtly political novel Robbins focuses attention upon the religious fanaticism that underlies so many of the world's troublesome problems.

Although Robbins sees religion as a "paramount contributor to human misery" (167), he by no means insists that it is the only source of people's woes. There are other distractions, "veils" of illusion, that obscure humanity's best purposes and goals. In each of the seven sections of *Skinny Legs and All*, Robbins strips away one of these veils with the expressed intention of affording his readers a glimpse of what he believes to be a deeper reality hidden beneath the surface of people's socially constructed lives. Since "humans erect institutions to conceal the unruly aspects of their own minds" (312), the reality that interests Robbins is to be found within an ancient room of the mind. This room is the "room of the wolfmother wallpaper" (1), the room in which Salome dances "the dance

of ultimate cognition, skinny legs and all" (2). The falling of the novel's
veils heralds Salome's famous dance, and in the final section of the book
many of its characters witness that dance for themselves—those characters, that is, who are not transfixed by the Super Bowl.

Some reviewers have described the passages where Robbins's narrator
gazes beyond the veils of self-deception as rather sermonlike. There is
no doubt that the ideas these passages address are central to their
writer's overall philosophy. In fact, as pointed out in Chapter 2, the metaphor of the veils handily incorporates all the major themes of Robbins's
six books. If, as reviewer Lee Lemon has observed, *Skinny Legs and All*
is indeed "part sermon," it is also "part love story, part fantasy, part
political novel, part satire" (Lemon 129). In any case, Robbins is a writer
interested in offering his readers a thoroughly entertaining novel of
ideas.

PLOT DEVELOPMENT

Readers might recognize Ellen Cherry Charles, protagonist of *Skinny
Legs and All*, as one of the Daughters of the Daily Special in *Jitterbug
Perfume*. In the earlier book, Ellen Cherry won an award that supported
her during six months of uninterrupted attention to her "true calling,"
landscape painting. When the work she produced ended up hanging in
a restaurant, she ruefully observed, "I escaped, my paintings didn't"
(24). In *Skinny Legs's* opening pages, readers learn that while the boost
provided by the Daughters assisted Ellen Cherry in launching a modest
career, she did not, in fact, break entirely free of the restaurant business.
She is happy enough, however, painting and working two shifts a week
at the War on Tuna Café when Boomer Petway, her hometown sweetheart, arrives in Seattle hoping to sweep her off her feet.

Boomer is successful in his enterprise, largely because he drives up to
Ellen Cherry's door in an immense mobile turkey. Not an artist himself
but a welder, Boomer nevertheless recognizes that art is the likeliest avenue to his beloved's heart. He has therefore applied his welder's torch
to the Airstream he inherited from his father, and the result is nothing
less than a "monument" to his love. The lover's strategem is an effective
one, the two immediately get married, and Ellen Cherry sees in the marriage an opportunity to escape the restaurant business forever. Because
Boomer is not particular about where he works as welder, the newly-

weds set forth in their turkey, heading for New York City, the mecca of the art world.

Robbins's account of the roast turkey's transcontinental voyage is a masterpiece of comic invention. Over hill and dale, the incongruous bird sails through the distinctive landscapes of the nation's heartland. As it "glides through the potato fields," the gigantic fowl necessarily inspires yearnings for a "flood of gravy" (17). In one particularly amusing scene, Ellen Cherry and Boomer decide to celebrate the one-week anniversary of their marriage by treating themselves to a triple feature at the drive-in movie theater in Livingston, Montana. "Hang the expense!" Boomer declares when he is charged for four parking spaces. (The bird takes up two lengthwise spaces, and another space on either side is "blocked by its drumsticks" [82].) Taking advantage of their parking arrangements, Boomer and Ellen Cherry enjoy *2020: So Who Needs Glasses?* in quadrophonic sound.

Besides delighting his readers with a remarkable exhibition of his genius for whim, Robbins uses the interval of the newlyweds' journey to provide useful background information and to set up certain features of his plot. For example, readers learn about Ellen Cherry's and Boomer's families and histories, about their early years in Colonial Pines, Virginia (a "suburb without an urb" [11]). When his Sunday sermon is received on the turkey's radio, readers are also introduced to the evangelistic Reverend Buddy Winkler, another resident of Colonial Pines and a figure well known to Boomer and Ellen Cherry. Throughout the course of the trip, readers witness Ellen Cherry's growing misgivings about her impulsive action. Realizing that her deepest commitment is to her art (about which her husband is decidedly disdainful), and that Boomer has in fact tricked her into the union, the new wife wonders how long the unlikely marriage will last.

Although Ellen Cherry and Boomer are in some respects an apparently ill-sorted pair, their sex life is deeply satisfying to them both. This being the case, the journey eastward is regularly punctuated by stops for their lovemaking. Robbins uses one of these stops, an occasion when the lovers take a picnic to a cave, to set in motion the fabulous adventures of five of *Skinny Legs*'s most extraordinary characters. Animated by the commotion the lustful humans have created, a pair of objects begins to stir in the nether regions of the cave. When they hear mysterious rustlings, Boomer and Ellen Cherry quickly gather their clothes together and flee to the welcome safety of their turkey. In their haste, they simply abandon a can of pork and beans, a silver spoon, and one of Boomer's purple socks.

Unbeknownst to the human characters, once again on their way to begin their new life, the things left behind in the cave are also eager to take to the road. When Can o' Beans, Spoon, and Dirty Sock notice that Painted Stick and Conch Shell, the original inhabitants of the cave, are actually able to move, they too discover in themselves the power of locomotion. Painted Stick and Conch Shell are both sacred relics; in ancient times they were instrumental in rituals honoring the great goddess Astarte. In their early days, these symbolic objects were witness to the building, destruction, and rebuilding of the famous temples of Jerusalem—now, sensing the advent of the Third Temple, they believe that the time has come to make their way back to Jerusalem. Having no other pressing plans, Can o' Beans, Spoon, and Sock agree to join Shell and Stick in their pilgrimage to the Holy City.

In granting a sense of selfhood to a collection of things, Robbins further extends the interest in objecthood he earlier expressed in *Still Life* and *Jitterbug Perfume*. All of his objects have distinctive personalities, seemingly shaped by various of their attributes or functions (Sock is somewhat coarse, Spoon delicate and shy). The objects are also gendered: the phallic stick is male, of course, and the pink and spiraled shell, nature's "calcified womb" (54), is known by the feminine pronoun. Being both container as well as thing contained, only Can o' Beans is at once a she and he. (Tiresias-like, Can o' Beans is much given to pursuit of knowledge and wisdom.) Using the voices that Robbins has bestowed upon them, *Skinny Legs*'s objects speak to the natures of the things in the world. The human being who does not attend to the nature of these things is, as Robbins's narrator succinctly puts it, an "animate chauvinist" (280).

The quest motif is once again at the heart of Robbins's plot. By the time the novel's third veil has fallen, its assorted characters are all to be found somewhere in New York. Having survived an exciting series of road adventures, the objects lurk in the basement of St. Patrick's Cathedral; there they await an opportunity to achieve their shared goal of eventually reaching Jerusalem. Another character also aspires to travel to Jerusalem, and his purpose is a deadly one. Ellen Cherry's Uncle Buddy Winkler wants to believe that the apocalypse is nigh. Designating himself the agent of Armageddon, Uncle Buddy plans to ignite World War III by blasting the Dome of the Rock, the mosque atop Jerusalem's

Temple Mount. In New York to raise money for his scheme, Uncle Buddy is at the center of an unholy and bloodthirsty alliance between fundamentalist Christians and radical Zionist Jews.

Meanwhile, a Jew and an Arab with a completely different goal in mind have opened a restaurant directly across from the United Nations plaza. Dedicating their enterprise to brotherhood, tolerance, and mutual understanding (but not, alas, to especially tasty food), Spike Cohen and Abu Hadee call their eatery Isaac & Ishmael's, after Abraham's Hebrew and Arab sons. That these amiable characters represent a live-and-let-live philosophy in more ways than one is revealed when readers learn that Spike is a shoe fetishist and that Abu's favorite pastime is washing dishes by hand. Engaged on a quest to promote harmony in the world, the two altogether accommodating eccentrics cheerfully rebuild their establishment each time it is bombed, acquire a giant-screen TV to satisfy their rabid football fans, and employ musicians and dancers on various special occasions. They also employ as a waitress Ellen Cherry Charles.

Yes, Ellen Cherry quickly finds herself back in the restaurant business. What was once her single-minded quest to seek personal fulfillment as an artist has become a far more complicated venture: disappointment has caused Ellen Cherry to question the roles that both art and love might play in her life, and thus she is a young woman in search of her own identity. Her first significant setback occurred when it was Boomer rather than she who became the overnight darling of New York's art world. After his turkey was sold to the Museum of Modern Art, Boomer turned his welder's skills to the production of other pieces of sculpture. An immediate success, the "upbeat redneck" with his "aloha shirts and new red beret" (177) sold every work in his first one-man show and was featured in *Vanity Fair*. Resentful and troubled about Boomer's new life, the "life that was supposed to have been *hers*" (183), Ellen Cherry begins to doubt her own vocation as artist.

Skinny Legs's protagonist suffers another personal setback when it turns out that it is Boomer who in fact leaves her. Having already envisioned the words that she would say after she had met a sympathetic fellow artist and found it necessary to gently shed her high-school sweetheart, Ellen Cherry is stunned to find that Boomer has dropped her. She is, moreover, astonished to discover that she truly misses her former lover and wishes to have him back. Boomer, however, who has "found him some other fish that he must fry," is unwilling to return while the subject of art lies "strictly taboo" (183) between them, and so Ellen

Cherry is left to struggle with her unresolved questions about the importance of art and love in her life while her estranged husband pursues his new career in the faraway city of Jerusalem.

Fortune is fickle in *Skinny Legs*'s plot. Thus Randolph (Boomer) Petway III is the character who almost effortlessly (and therefore maddeningly) realizes the goals that other characters earnestly strive to achieve. It is he who reaches Jerusalem long before the objects have managed to find their way, and it is he who fully enjoys the sense of artistic accomplishment that has long been Ellen Cherry's goal. Neither of these objectives has been central to Boomer's own aspirations; in fact, his life's goal is seemingly achieved when he marries Ellen Cherry. However, as he is later forced to admit, he cannot feel truly wedded to her as long as she thinks of herself as married to her art. Therefore, Boomer's ultimate quest is to win the love and respect of the woman he adores, and his initial foray into the world of art is dedicated to that end. When he discovers that creating art is actually fun, albeit in a "useless sort of way" (203), he readily embraces this new dimension of experience. Boomer, after all, has always been fond of having fun.

Left to stew in her own miseries, and therefore having little fun, Ellen Cherry waits tables, searches for a new lover, worries about her Uncle Buddy's nefarious activities, and struggles to overcome her painting block. For a time she seriously considers abandoning her painting altogether, but its hold on her is strong. When a rush of inspiration finally seizes her, she produces a mural for Isaac & Ishmael's. A painting that is dramatic in "its complexity, its nocturnal richness," Ellen Cherry's interior landscape presents a scene that is, as the novel's narrator observes, "not unlike . . . the room of the wolfmother wallpaper" (374). While the regular patrons of the restaurant offer decidedly mixed responses to the mural, Ellen Cherry's work inspires Salome, Isaac & Ishmael's popular belly dancer, to at last agree to dance the Dance of the Seven Veils.

Anticipation and excitement characterize the scenes that lead up to Salome's climactic dance. For the characters of *Skinny Legs and All*, there is the suggestion of the apocalyptic in the air. On the one hand, Ellen Cherry grows increasingly apprehensive about the Reverend Buddy Winkler's evil plans. While working at Isaac & Ishmael's, Ellen Cherry has learned a great deal about the political problems of the Middle East, a region she earlier envisioned as simply the source of ornate rugs. Not only is Uncle Buddy the kind of dangerous egomaniac who might well succeed in triggering an immense catastrophe, she worries, but he also seems determined to enmesh Boomer in his plot. Ellen Cherry therefore notifies both the FBI and the Southern Baptist Convention of the fanatical preacher's monstrous intentions.

Within the more localized domain of Isaac & Ishmael's, the atmosphere, on the other hand, is charged with a different kind of tension. Salome's long-awaited dance promises to offer its observers some special form of revelation, but the restaurant's faithful following has an important decision to make. Salome has scheduled her performance for Super Bowl Sunday, and she plans to begin to dance right around kickoff time. Spike and Abu are willing to sponsor both activities, for they can move their television screen out into the courtyard, but seating will be limited, and restaurant patrons will all have to make their choice. For the fans who have a special stake in the fortunes of the hometown favorites, the decision will be a particularly difficult one—this season a New York team has made it to the Super Bowl.

While various of *Skinny Legs*'s human characters await opportunity to express their fanaticism (Robbins clearly delights in the fact that *fan*, as in football *fan*, is short for *fanatic*), the objects gathered in St. Patrick's Cathedral agree that the time has come to resume their journey to Jerusalem. Although Spoon and Painted Stick have earlier sallied forth in attempts to locate suitable means of transportation, they have not met with success during their adventure-filled excursions. (Indeed, Spoon spent some time with Ellen Cherry, who was thoroughly bewildered by the sudden appearance of an object that so closely resembled the spoon she had thought to be forever lost. Having experienced a mystical moment while gazing intently at the object so inexplicably restored to her possession, Ellen Cherry is inspired to paint Spoon's image in her mural.)[1]

Eventually, all the objects but Dirty Sock reach their destination. Riding on Conch Shell's back, Can o' Beans makes his/her way by traveling through the ocean—a thrilling experience, but one that naturally leaves him/her terribly rusted. Through a serendipitous sequence of events, Painted Stick and Spoon manage to travel by boat, for these objects have hidden themselves in a package of "Armageddon paraphernalia" (421) that Uncle Buddy has shipped off to Boomer. As for Dirty Sock, he must be content to observe a world of passing feet from the basement window of St. Patrick's.

Sunday, January 23, turns out to be a day that changes many people's lives. Salome's spectacularly enlightening dance lasts through the duration of the Super Bowl; those who are present enter the room of the wolfmother wallpaper via a "dance floor of ideas" (413), and with every purple veil that falls, a vision of an enlarged reality emerges for those gathered in the room. The last veil is the one that masks Salome's beautiful face, and when it flies away, and the dancer spins solitary and naked before the crowd, Ellen Cherry understands about reality in its final and grandest sense that *"Everybody's got to figure it out for themselves"* (412). When she resolves to try to figure it out for herself, Ellen Cherry flies to Jerusalem for a reunion with Boomer.

Sunday, the day he had intended to demolish the Dome of the Rock, is the Reverend Buddy Winkler's last day, the day of his personal Armageddon. Representatives of the CIA have indeed taken an interest in Uncle Buddy, and after a brief visit with him, they have confiscated his passport. Frustrated at having been thwarted just before his shining hour, Buddy needs an "outlet for the righteous energy, the redemptive fury" (410) that rage within a fanatic's heart. He therefore sets out for Isaac & Ishmael's, arriving just after Salome has completed her last pirouette. When he grabs her by her throat, Uncle Buddy is shot dead.

Other lives are changed as well. Salome, wounded in the melee, will never dance again at Isaac & Ishmael's. When she has recovered sufficiently for travel, the young Jewish-Arab girl goes home to the Middle East. Detective Jackie Shaftoe, also wounded in the gunfire, retires from the police department and devotes his days to painting. Once an avid football fan, Shaftoe never watches a game again. Of course, few in New York are aware of the fate of one fanatical zealot or of the events that transformed the lives of those who participated in the Dance of the Seven Veils. The pandemonium in the city's streets signals New York's victory in the Super Bowl!

As in his other novels, Robbins employs a variety of narrative strategies in the telling of his tale. Interestingly, readers enter *Skinny Legs and All* through the gateway offered by its "prelude," a short and lyrical passage filled with imagery at once familiar and strange. The prelude is intended to draw readers into "the room of the wolfmother wallpaper," and thus the novel's narrative voice issues invitation through its use of direct address (wherein the reader is called "you"). Although the prelude is the only part of Robbins's fifth book that makes use of direct address, his experiment with second-person point of view anticipates the narrative strategy he will later fully employ in *Half Asleep in Frog Pajamas*.

The narrator's use of direct address, and with it the present tense, distinguishes the prelude, setting it off from the story that is largely told from a third-person, past-tense point of view. It is by clearly setting off this passage that Robbins is able to purposefully use it as a point of entry not into the plot itself, but into the novel, the novel as seen as a work of art. The use of the prelude as a portal to the novel and its ideas is thus analogous to the book's depiction of Salome's dance as a point of entry for Ellen Cherry and the others into a world of revelations. *Skinny Legs* offers another example, a particularly vivid one, of the use of this device: when the narrator describes Ellen Cherry's mural, the reader is informed that "the viewer's eye entered the painting through the beak of an owl" (373). In similar fashion, the prelude serves as the owl's beak through which the novel itself is entered.

While *Skinny Legs*'s story is highly entertaining, this book is also strikingly a novel of ideas. Issues relating to religion, art, politics, and economy are among those thrown open to debate within its pages. Because Robbins well understands that the narrator who frequently engages in philosophical speculation runs the risk of diverting readers' attention away from the "narrative flow" (99)[2] of the story's action, he uses voices other than the narrator's to pose many of the provocative questions that the novel raises. Particularly useful in this respect are the five objects brought to life as characters. Each of the objects has observed the realm of human activity from a distinct perspective, and each therefore has an idiosyncratic opinion to contribute to their ongoing conversation (while traveling and hiding in the cathedral, the objects talk a great deal among themselves). In an important way, then, these unusual characters function as mouthpieces through which ideas relevant to the novel's action can be expressed in an engaging fashion.

The narrator's voice is once again that of the omniscient storyteller. Like that of the narrator of *Jitterbug Perfume*, this voice offers commentary on the characters and developments of plot and occasionally presages events that are to come. While the narrator frequently proffers witticisms or engages in other forms of verbal play, there are also passages that resonate with the intensity of strong conviction. As is perhaps befitting the subject matter of the novel, the narrative voice is often distinctly wry in tone.

CHARACTERS

Among the sensitive issues that *Skinny Legs* explores is the question of how people who are very different from one another might live in harmony together. To dramatize this problem, Robbins presents readers with several sets of characters who can be regarded as contrasting pairs. Some of the novel's characters manage to bridge the gulfs that lie between them, but others unquestionably do not. Spike and Abu, with their different ethnic loyalties and heritages, are an obvious example of a contrasting pair. Despite their many differences, including their quirky fascinations (for shoes or dishwater in their respective cases), these characters share a common ground. Spike and Abu decided to go into business together after they both attended a peace rally; the common ground they share is their belief in tolerance and acceptance of the differences of others. The full measure of their acceptance of others can perhaps be seen in the trouble they take to accommodate both Salome and the football fans—who clearly share no common ground.

In sharp contrast to the philosophy espoused by the owners of Isaac & Ishmael's is that preached by the Reverend Buddy Winkler. There is no generosity of spirit in the judgmental and retributory message that Uncle Buddy bears. In fact, Bud longs for the end of time so that he can prove that he is right where others have been wrong. In *Skinny Legs*'s plot, Uncle Buddy plays the role of the doomsayer, the killjoy, the apocalytic voice that prophesies disaster. Since his primary role is that of sounding the trumpet of doom, his voice is indeed the Reverend Buddy's most outstanding feature. "Reminiscent of a saxophone," Bud's mesmerizing voice is "fecund and round and gloomily romantic" (7). Those of Buddy's following who only know him as a radio voice are naturally unaware that if his melodic voice often seems to belie his monstrous nature, his appearance certainly does not: the fanatic's "lean and hungry" (7) face is inflamed with angry-looking pustules and boils.

The apocalyptic vision that is personified in the character of Uncle Buddy is also represented by Salome's sixth veil. As Robbins earlier suggested in *Another Roadside Attraction*, the allure of a belief in a final day of judgment can be seductive and strong. Nevertheless, such a belief is revealed to be one of *Skinny Legs*'s veils of self-deception, and when the sixth veil has fallen, it is clear that "to emphasize the afterlife is to deny life" (305) itself. The novel's account of the life and times of the Reverend Buddy Winkler serves to underscore this point. Relegating his hope for happiness to the time of the hereafter, Bud spends his living days angrily proclaiming, denouncing, and scheming. Finally, in his last act of self-righteous fury, he foolishly squanders his very being. Uncle Buddy's entire career is thus devoted to his denial of the value of living. As one who rejects the possibilities of life, Bud shares no common ground with Spike and Abu, characters who cherish their daily existence.

Ellen Cherry and Boomer are another contrasting pair, and much of the plot is focused upon their efforts to find the common ground for their marriage. Their mutual sexual attraction is strong, but a meeting of minds is necessary to bridge the differences that separate them. Their marked differences in attitude and style—Ellen Cherry is a serious and purposeful young woman while Boomer is a happy-go-lucky, wisecracking, beer-guzzling sort of fellow—are only exacerbated when their conversation turns to art, the subject that is most serious of all to Ellen Cherry. When Boomer's playfully conceived sculptures attract serious attention, Ellen Cherry cannot help but feel that what has happened is not fair. Naturally she is ashamed of the resentment that she harbors, but she cannot deny that the differences in their attitudes toward art have in fact come between them.

Ellen Cherry's sense of herself as an artist is central to her identity. Her habit of seeing the world "from a different perspective" (15) originated in her childhood when, to combat her car sickness, she would lie in the back of the family station wagon and play her special "eye game." By squinting in various ways, Ellen Cherry could view interesting juxtapositions of features of the landscape or even make herself color-blind. Her interest in art further developed during her school days, when she was always the child who could draw better than anyone else in her class. When she moved to Seattle, Ellen Cherry completed a degree in art at the Cornish College of the Arts.

It was her desire to pursue her interest in art that impelled Ellen Cherry to move all the way to Seattle, but the event that necessitated her leaving Colonial Pines gave shape to another feature of her sense of her own identity. Ellen Cherry is fascinated by the biblical figure Jezebel. In fact, she thinks of Jezebel as "her eternal double, her familiar" (22), as it were. This conception of herself arose out of the greatest humiliation Ellen Cherry ever suffered, one that was largely the handiwork of Uncle Buddy Winkler. After she left high school, Ellen Cherry began art studies at Virginia Commonwealth University in the nearby city of Richmond. When rumors reached Colonial Pines that nude models posed for VCU's students, Bud persuaded Ellen Cherry's father to join him in protest of this outrage. The two men burst into Ellen Cherry's class and dragged her from the room. Then, chanting "Jezebel" over and over, they scrubbed the makeup from her face. Since the day of this degrading episode, Ellen Cherry has puzzled over that what it was that Jezebel did to warrant the enduring hostility of men.

If Boomer is at first uncomfortable with Ellen Cherry's role as artist, he is also made uneasy by her identification with Jezebel. When they are making love in the cave, Ellen Cherry requests that her husband call her by that name. Deeply reluctant to do so, Boomer finally halfheartedly agrees—and it is when they hear that old familiar name invoked that Painted Stick and Conch Shell at once begin to stir. (Although they have no opportunity to converse with Ellen Cherry, Stick and Shell know the answer to her question: Jezebel's fault in the eyes of men is that she too was a devotee of the great goddess Astarte.)

Although Boomer has some trouble accepting certain elements of Ellen Cherry's nature, he truly loves his wife, and it is out of his wish to understand her better that he undertakes his own odyssey into her special world, that of the artist.[3] Before he establishes his unexpected reputation as a sculptor, Boomer is a high school dropout whose favorite pastime is reading spy novels. When he becomes a celebrity, he begins to feel that he is actually something of a spy himself, or, as he puts it, "an undercover agent. A mole in the house of art" (203). There is no doubt, however, that he rapidly develops a strong commitment to his new interest, and his surprising fervor sets in motion the role reversal that he and Ellen Cherry unhappily undergo: whereas it was once Boomer who was leery of Ellen Cherry's commitment to her passion, changed circumstances leave Ellen Cherry uncomfortable with Boomer's role as artist.

In the end Ellen Cherry and Boomer do find common ground in the very field that has seemed to lie between them. Just as Boomer comes to an understanding of Ellen Cherry's artist's passion, she comes to an appreciation of his artful playfulness. Boomer is the figure in *Skinny Legs* who carries Robbins's recurrent message, his general advice to "lighten up," and this theme is clearly reflected in the sculptures that he fashions. The turkey, of course, was an unwitting expression of the theme, but with the piece he constructs in Jerusalem Boomer makes a fully self-conscious statement. His sculpture, meant to jar Arabs and Jews out of taking themselves too seriously, depicts the ancient trickster god Pales (after whom, readers are told, Palestine was named). Pales is a fabulous figure, part human and part donkey, part female and part male. Once venerated by both Hebrews and Arabs, who relied upon wild asses for survival in the desert, Pales speaks to the common roots of the Middle Eastern peoples. Boomer hopes that his "goofy and vulgar" (365) sculpture will remind Arabs and Jews that they share a common ground. Ellen Cherry, who knows "what works on an aesthetic level," has to admit that "as nutty as this piece is, as a work of art it ain't bad" (365).

Like the others of the novel's characters, the five objects also represent contrasting positions. Painted Stick and Conch Shell are the artifacts of a very ancient culture; Spoon, Sock, and Can o' Beans belong to the modern world. Brought together by the circumstance of their common pilgrimage, the objects constitute a party not altogether unlike—though much smaller than—the diverse assemblage depicted by Geoffrey Chaucer in the *Canterbury Tales*. (Like Chaucer's characters, the objects debate cultural issues and tell stories about themselves.) Stick and Shell embody the male and female principles that are unified in a mother goddess cult, and Sock and Spoon represent differing aspects of their contemporary, paternalistic society—the male Sock is a secular figure, loud-mouthed and opinionated, while the female Spoon is demure and thoroughly devout, having served as a utensil in a pious Catholic household. As the sage, the seeker of wisdom, Can o' Beans serves as moderator for the unlikely group. When Can o' Beans finally reaches Jerusalem, he/she appropriately finds a final resting place at the foot of Boomer's monument to the Middle East's ancient (and also androgynous) trickster.

Most of Robbins's novels include a representative of the archetypal earth-mother goddess, and in *Skinny Legs and All*, Salome is that figure. (Of course, in her secret identification with Jezebel the novel's protagonist is also linked to the feminine life force.) The mysterious and sensuous Salome seems to possess a deep and hidden wisdom—the ancient knowledge of the serpent. Her movements suggest both "a bright creative power and a dark destructive power" (301), the aspects of Astarte, in whose tradition she dances. Set in contrast to Salome and the revelations offered by her dancing is the contemporary phenomenon of football fanaticism. The cult of Astarte was supplanted by the monotheistic, patriarchal religions, and the novel makes clear that the cult of football can be seen as the most recent formulation of yet another patriarchal religion.

STYLE

One of *Skinny Legs and All*'s epigraphs succinctly captures the atmosphere of Robbins's fifth book. It reads:

IT'S THE END OF THE WORLD AS WE KNOW IT (AND I
FEEL FINE).
—R.E.M.

Tom Robbins's characteristic flair for unfolding his phantasmagorical tale in the spirit of exuberant hilarity is clearly evident in this book (which, after all, opens with the launching of its magnificent and monstrous turkey). Robbins is still undeniably the writer who, as reviewer Steven Dougherty once described him, "dips history's pigtails in weird ink and splatters his graffiti over the face of modern fiction . . . who fingerpaints the great themes" (Dougherty 123). Nevertheless, in *Skinny Legs* the writer is intent upon situating his novel's picaresque adventures within the context of quite serious current and present political dangers (those fermenting in the Middle East) and within the milieu of an end-of-time mentality (the apocalyptic vision). Thus, as his epigraph declares, Robbins wishes to affirm his comic view of time in defiance of his age's threats of catastrophe.

Uncle Buddy clearly serves as the novel's active voice of doom and as the immediate locus of danger in respect to the problems of the Middle East, but his is not a voice crying in the wilderness, and therefore Robbins employs several stylistic devices to create a strong sense of the atmosphere in which a character like Uncle Buddy moves. (Uncle Buddy is both a creature of his times and a leader whose voice commands the attention of numerous sympathetic followers. His message addresses the political uncertainties and the fundamentalist sentiments that exist within the land, and the writer wishes to insist upon the presence of these uncertainties and sentiments.)

Many of Robbins's techniques are almost cinematic, as when Ellen Cherry and Boomer repeatedly hear news accounts of deaths in the Middle East over the radio in their turkey—or when they see signs along the highway warning that the day of judgment is nigh. After they have completed their transcontinental journey, they ruminate upon the fact that all of America has seemed to have been obsessed with a sense of finality, as reflected in people's worried talk about AIDS and the Middle East. Even the name of the event currently on the minds of sports fanatics hints at a preoccupation with the end—ominously, the basketball tournament is called The *Final* Four. Later, Ellen Cherry's eye falls upon grim headlines in one of New York's newspapers (more conflicts in the Middle East), and Boomer's letters to her recount his own observations of the troubles in Jerusalem. All of these references to circumstances that hint of the imminence of cataclysmic events signal the spirit of the times, and Robbins uses them to serve as backdrop for the central action of his novel.

THEME

Skinny Legs's use of the conceit of the seven veils provides Robbins with an opportunity to recapitulate the major themes of his fiction in a comprehensive fashion. This novel's recasting of earlier themes emphatically includes the writer's characteristic critiques of such powerful institutions as politics, organized religion, and the marketplace. Besides revisiting his persistent concerns about the workings of these dominant social forces, Robbins insists on the idea that the individual is ultimately responsible for directly engaging in the shaping of reality, a point that he particularly stressed in *Even Cowgirls Get the Blues*. Ellen Cherry Charles, like Sissy Hankshaw, finds that every individual must "establish his or her own special, personal, particular, unique, direct, one-on-one, hands-on relationship with . . . the universe" (412). The recurrence of these central themes throughout the body of Robbins's work is fully outlined in chapter 2.

By structuring his novel's events around the falling of each separate veil, the writer is able to vividly dramatize what he sees as the significant repercussions of living with certain of the illusions supported and perpetuated by social institutions. Perhaps the most serious of these repercussions occurs when anthropocentric human beings reject nature, reject "the living present, the living planet—in order to chase after a transcendent goal" (304). In focusing too intently upon the abstract value of power over others, existence in the afterlife, or possession of the dollar, politics, organized religion, and the marketplace overlook or justify the acts of warfare and destruction, pollution, persecution, and ruthless competition that mar enjoyment of the wonders of "the living planet." In part, the objects' presence in the novel serves as a reminder that things, as well as human beings, are part of the natural world. The references to Astarte and a mother goddess cult suggest a time when practice of religion was a celebration of the centrality of human beings' connection to the earth. Using the example of this ancient tradition to illustrate how humanity itself is a "function of nature," the novel argues that humanity cannot "live in opposition to nature except in a schizophrenic crime" (404). If Ellen Cherry and the others of *Skinny Legs*'s characters are indeed living out their lives, as the novel's atmosphere suggests, in the last days of the world, then it is likely that the coming apocalypse will be the result of humanity's crimes against nature and thus against itself.

When the veils that represent humankind's schizophrenic impulses to repress the natural world finally fall away, both readers and the novel's characters find themselves in the special room of the mind that is first depicted in *Skinny Legs*'s prelude. The room of the "wolfmother wallpaper," the "toadstool motel" (1), is always presented in images that juxtapose human artifacts (wallpaper or motel) with the things that belong to the earth itself (wolfmother and toadstool). Indeed, Ellen Cherry's mural offers this same juxtaposition: there stars and furniture are brought together, and mascara jars and crickets. The little silver spoon bounces on a buffalo hide. Vibrating with the living presence of the concrete objects of the world, neither the mural nor the landscape of the room within the mind seems to hint of any need for some transcendent goal. Rather, the room of the wolfmother wallpaper speaks to the immediacy of being. In this room the self is at one with the natural world, at one with the existence of the universe.

Most of Robbins's novels present readers with multiple themes to consider, and *Skinny Legs and All* is certainly no exception. Given its protagonist's central preoccupation, it is not surprising that the book offers reflections on the nature of art. In an especially delightful passage, *Skinny Legs*'s narrator addresses this subject by rhapsodizing over the astonishing artistry of the common mockingbird. Readers are informed that although the mockingbird is born with a marvelously intricate song of its own, it is not satisfied to rest upon its laurels. The mockingbird is a true artist, and therefore it is intent upon rearranging reality. By gathering fragments of birdsong from the entire bird kingdom, the mockingbird builds a repertoire from which it can create new and unexpected arrangements or surprising juxtapositions of notes and motifs. Its artistry lies in its ability to re-create the world from the world itself, and this is precisely what Ellen Cherry does when she plays her special "eye game" or produces a landscape that presents a world made new in the design of her own shaping.

The subject of art comes up once again when Boomer questions Ellen Cherry about what it is that the artist does. At this point Boomer has sold his turkey, and his agent has suggested that she would like to market additional examples of his sculptures. As yet, however, Boomer has not self-consciously set out to produce a work of art, and he is befuddled by the problem of not knowing how he might begin. He wonders if artists' inspirations occur to them in dreams. When Ellen Cherry explains that the process is usually not that exotic, that the artist simply wishes to see something as it has not been seen before, Boomer immediately understands how he should proceed. He realizes that there are many things he would like to take a "gander at," but that he has never seen these things because the world does not offer them "in stock" (180). To see the things he wants to see he will have to create them for himself.

As indicated in the example of the mockingbird, the artist's creative act gives shape to a rearranging of reality. While Ellen Cherry quickly grows disillusioned with the New York art scene, where people pose and strut and engage in superficial talk of money, she does find an artist whom she can admire. Turn Around Norman is a street artist, a man who is dedicated to rearranging reality by moving imperceptibly. Norman spends his days in one spot, moving without seeming to. The observer will never detect Norman's motion, but after a short time has elapsed, Norman can be perceived to be pointed in a new direction. (Norman's minimalist art form suggests the ordinary condition of objecthood, and indeed the five objects are fascinated by this human being's unusual performance.)

Skinny Legs's vision of art as the creative enterprise that renews nature by constantly rearranging its realities emphasizes the productive relationship between the artist and the world. Set in sharp contrast to its artists' several and varied acts of re-creation (in song, painting, sculpture, dance, and movement) is the novel's depiction of the destructive designs of an imagination such as that of the Reverend Buddy Winkler—whose relationship to the world is never productive. Held in thrall by his apocalyptic death wish, Uncle Buddy would far sooner destroy than create.

Of course, Tom Robbins is also an artist who is interested in rearranging reality and to that end blends the comic with the satiric to produce a novel that is at once both entertaining and thought-provoking. *Skinny Legs*'s special rearrangement of reality presents a world wherein an object can assert its own presence and identity and the mockingbird can be celebrated as an artist extraordinaire. When the book conjures into being the room of the wolfmother wallpaper, it juxtaposes the private reality of personal cognition with the social realities of the public world portrayed in its story's plot. Like the visions of the artists whose work is described, Robbins's idiosyncratic perspective provides an entirely fresh look at the world.

ALTERNATE READING: THE PERSPECTIVE OF
CULTURAL STUDIES

Because *Skinny Legs and All* presents its own critique of certain contemporary cultural institutions, it seems appropriate to consider the
novel in the context of cultural studies, a relatively new and broad field
of inquiry that encourages analysis of sites of meaning and power within
societies. Over the last thirty years or so, cultural criticism has supported
investigation of all conceivable aspects of social/cultural experience in
the spirit of identifying and naming that which is meaningful in the lives
that people live. Described by such critics as Richard Hoggart or Stuart
Hall as a field of studies rather than a well-defined discipline, cultural
criticism is committed to exploration of the multifaceted nature of cultures and their networks of interconnected social institutions. Beginning
with the work of Raymond Williams, cultural critics have assumed that
how a society lives, what it believes, and what it produces are all worthy
of inquiry; the act of analyzing and interpreting the multiple artifacts
wherein a society represents itself can reveal much about its people and
the institutions they have erected.

In appreciating the work of Turn Around Norman, whose street art is
presented in the arena of popular culture, Ellen Cherry supports one of
the main tenets of cultural studies, that which argues that defining a
society in the light of the values represented by its so-called "high culture" is insufficient, indeed contradictory, to the task of identifying much
of that which has significance within people's lives. Cultural critics
therefore work to break down the boundaries that have in the past separated popular culture from high culture. In this effort, they oppose an
elitist attitude that would either denigrate or sentimentalize the representations of what has been called popular culture. Their position is
grounded in the view that society itself is composed of multiple, inter-
active, and constantly changing elements of cultural significance, and is
therefore too complex to be represented only in an abstract ideal of a
high culture. Ellen Cherry, therefore, does not distinguish Norman's art
from that which is traditionally housed in famous museums; for her,
Norman's performance exists within the context of *Skinny Legs*'s definition of art as the act of rearranging reality (an act that Norman ever so
subtly achieves.)

The objects brought to life are all cultural artifacts, and it is interesting
to speculate about the novel's use of them as instruments of represen-

tation. Conch Shell and Painted Stick are both natural objects that have been appropriated for symbolic use in human rituals. (Interestingly, Stick's cultural purpose is signified by the coat of paint that distinguishes him from other sticks in the world, but Shell's purpose is implicit in her shape and in the context of her relation to Stick.) It is likely that it strikes the reader as thoroughly appropriate that as representations of an earth goddess cult these artifacts are themselves natural objects of the earth and that their shapes speak to the principles of procreation central to that cult. Furthermore, their use as sacred objects has understandably imbued them with the magical properties they possess.

If Spoon, Sock, and Can o' Beans at first appear quite pedestrian when compared with the exotic relics they encounter, it is *Skinny Legs's* purpose to show how they, too, are meaningful (and, in fact, how they can also be perceived as magical). The American artifacts are all manufactured and thus represent a culture whose relation to the earth is obviously quite different from that emblematized by the natural objects. (In fact, Can o' Beans is quite conscious of the fact that he/she is likely to become litter in the natural landscape.) As objects that are manufactured, made rather than appropriated, the modern artifacts are seemingly a step removed from the natural environment to which Shell and Stick are intrinsically linked. Nevertheless, these objects belong to a world that has been re-created, a world whose reality has in fact been rearranged, and in its conception of the room of the wolfmother wallpaper, where cultural artifacts are conjoined with the features of the "living planet," the novel celebrates the meaningfulness of objecthood. In their own ways, Spoon, Dirty Sock, and Can o' Beans all represent characteristics of the culture that has produced them.

A society's products can be regarded as representations of aspects of its culture, but cultural critics are also interested in the ways in which concepts exist as representations. *Skinny Legs* offers an interesting example of this in its discussion of AIDS. For Buddy Winkler and his followers, the idea of the apocalypse is reified in the phenomenon of AIDS. This epidemic, as the narrator notes, is "tailor-made" (330) for those who seek proof that the end is at hand. The Reverend Winkler equates AIDS with sin because his representation of it focuses upon the fact that it can be transmitted through the sexual act. (Of course, this particular representation excludes the understanding that AIDS can also be transmitted in other ways as well.) From the point of linking AIDS with sin it is but a short step for the Reverend Winkler to infer that humanity's days are numbered, for AIDS results in death, and, as he believes, death is appropriately the wages of sin. *Skinny Legs*'s analysis of Winkler's thinking presents readers with a thoughtful example of cultural criticism at work.

NOTES

1. While trying to overcome her painting block, Ellen Cherry departs from her usual practice of focusing on landscapes. Her Warhol-like portraits of a silver spoon, a purple sock, and a can of beans reflect memories of ecstasy in a cave and suggest that she is no "animate chauvinist."

2. One of the objects actually comments on the necessity of preserving the integrity of the narrative line. Listening to Conch Shell and Painted Stick relate the story of the building of Jerusalem's First Temple, Can o' Beans would like to interrupt with questions that occur during the course of the telling; however, he/she also wants to hear the story to its end, and therefore does not dare disrupt the "narrative flow."

3. Although Ellen Cherry does not know it, the first work of art Boomer intentionally sets out to make is designed with her in mind. Boomer's creation is a gigantic spy's trenchcoat in which he has sewn five hundred hidden pockets. In these pockets are five hundred secret messages written in five hundred different codes. When decoded, each message reads: "Randolph Petway III loves Ellen Cherry Charles" (183).

Half Asleep in Frog Pajamas
(1994)

Whether life is serious or just trivial, I haven't a clue.
—August Strindberg, *The Dance of Death*

The catastrophe that seemed so imminent in *Skinny Legs and All* is indeed depicted in Robbins's sixth novel. The action of *Half Asleep in Frog Pajamas* opens on Maundy Thursday, which is in this novel the fateful day when the American stock market resoundingly collapses. By envisioning his disaster in the form of an economic calamity, Tom Robbins creates occasion to put to the test nothing less than the traditional American dream of extravagant material success. In this novel's landscape the omnipresent poor have long since lost the capacity to dream the dream of easy street—hordes of them are living a hard life on the sidewalks of the streets. Therefore, the question sardonically posed by the novel's plot is centered upon the lot of the upwardly mobile middle class: whatever will become of the dreams of those who are poised to secure the good life, those who still owe payments on their Rolexes and Porsches?

To answer the question, the story focuses on what promises to be the worst weekend in the short life of Gwendolyn Mati, an ambitious commodities broker. *Frog Pajamas*'s protagonist is something of a prissy Madonna, a thoroughly "material girl," but one who is not much interested in her own sexual nature. (As a professional commodities dealer, she is well aware, however, of the value of sex as commodity.) The untimely market crash means trouble for Gwen, who has engaged in questionable business practices. In fact, as she candidly admits, "I've left my clients so far underwater, they're going to need gills to breathe" (3). Unless Monday morning's reopening of the market brings a significant rally, the desperate broker's underhanded maneuverings are bound to come to light. With her job in jeopardy and her many payments coming due, Gwen must wait out the long Easter weekend to learn whether it will seem possible that her materialist dream can be resurrected.

In *Skinny Legs and All*, Salome's fifth veil represented the illusion that is made manifest when money, which handily serves as a marker in life's game, becomes confused with the playing of the game itself (*Skinny Legs* 231). Gwen Mati is clearly someone who has subscribed to this illusion. She has hoped that if she could play her cards right, then the markers that she would surely accumulate would serve to affirm the value of her life. What she does not know, when her frantic weekend begins, is that the deck of cards with which she has been playing is about to be changed: the deck at hand is the tarot deck, and the card that keeps coming up for Gwen is the one that signifies the Fool.

The narrative voice in *Frog Pajamas* speaks directly to its protagonist, always addressing Gwen Mati as "you." In other words, this voice relates to Gwen—whether she is listening or not—an account of her own experiences, thoughts, words, and encounters with others as they occur in the present tense: " 'This is the worst day of my life,' you say, as you drop a salted peanut into your double martini—on better days, you drink white wine" (3). Various writers, including Ernest Hemingway, Robert Penn Warren, and John Dos Passos, have been known to embed second-person passages in their essentially first- or third-person narratives to achieve certain stylistic effects (the use of "you" generalizes experience, rendering it as typical for everyone). These writers' occasional employment of the second person for rhetorical purposes resembles Robbins's own use of the technique in *Skinny Legs and All*. In *Frog Pajamas*, where Robbins sustains second-person narration throughout the course of the novel, the story's mode of telling is at the heart of its fictional structure.

The consistent use of a second-person narrative strategy places the reader in an unusual position, one that is inherently ambiguous. Does the novelistic voice that addresses "you" speak, in the fullest sense of its effect, to the fictional protagonist, to the reader, or to both? The ambiguity in second-person viewpoint is, as literary theorist Ronald Fraser notes, made especially apparent when this perspective is compared with that of the first-person point of view. There the reader is presented the account of an "I" whose position is either accepted or rejected. (The "I" whom the reader cannot believe is usually called the "unreliable" narrator.) As Fraser points out, "what cannot be done" in an instance of this kind "is to suspend belief and at the same time to believe" (Fraser 64). Interestingly, however, it is precisely this seemingly paradoxical condition that is effected with the use of "you." While *Frog Pajamas*'s reader understands that Gwen Mati is the ostensible "you" toward whom the novel's attention is directed, this reader is also aware that she or he occupies the position of the "you" vis-à-vis the viewpoint embodied by the protagonist. Thus, Fraser argues, "at one and the same time it is you [the reader] and not you who is being addressed" (Fraser 65).

The ambiguity of the reader's position in the second-person narrative might be further explored by considering how the reader feels about her or his relation to the world of the novel. A second-person strategy seems to dramatize the role of the reading audience, to suggest that the reader plays some part in the conditions of the story's telling. The reader might feel as though she or he were being addressed in the persona of Gwen Mati (occupying, that is, the protagonist's role in the novel), or the reader might feel rather like an eavesdropper, someone whose presence is implied, someone who is overhearing the speech that is directed to another. In *Frog Pajamas* it is likely that the reader's position will be defined by the degree of sympathy she or he is willing to extend to the protagonist at various moments in the novel. In any case, Robbins's narrative technique serves to implicate his reader in the text while his concomitant use of the present tense creates the effect of a story that seems to be unfolded, revealed, or shown rather than recounted: the reader distinctly experiences the you-are-there sensation.

As noted earlier, Tom Robbins is a writer who is interested in experimenting with narrative technique. (Chapters 3 and 4 examine the writer's innovative use of variations of the third-person point of view, and chapter 7 describes how Robbins uses direct address in *Skinny Legs*'s prelude to distinguish that section of the book from the rest of the novel.) It was perhaps while he was writing *Skinny Legs* that Robbins conceived the idea of fully employing the second-person narrator in a subsequent work of fiction. While this strategy is not without precedent, its occurrence, nevertheless, is relatively rare. Jay McInerney used it in his *Bright Lights, Big City* (1984) first novel, and Michel Butor earlier employed it in his highly regarded *A Change of Heart* (1957).[1] In common with *Half Asleep in Frog Pajamas*, these other two novels feature a narrative voice that speaks to a main character who is undergoing a journey toward self-revelation. Through the intimacy of direct address, the reader shares both the adventures of the journey and the experience of revelation.

Because the narrative strategy employed in *Frog Pajamas* is admittedly uncommon, readers might find it quite noticeable at first. As one reviewer remarked about his reading experience, "either you get used to [it], as I did, or find [it] enormously irritating, which I did also" (Elbling 11). Generally speaking, readers quickly adjust to the novelty of the second-person perspective and find, as did Wayne Booth when he read Butor's book, that "it is surprising how quickly one is absorbed into the illusory 'present' of the story" (Booth 150). Nevertheless, the second-person narrative is unusual enough that it does call attention to itself and can therefore be seen as a device that might be used by a writer to defamiliarize the act of narration. Robbins has, on other occasions, employed narrative techniques that serve to remind his readers that the novel is a construct; his use of just such a device in *Frog Pajamas* could perhaps explain the reviewer's mixed response to the novel's narrative mode, one that might strike some readers as seeming too intrusively an artifice.

Unconventional though it is, the second-person narrative offers certain advantages to the writer of the novel. For one thing, its you-are-there effect well suits the cinematic style of Robbins's episodic plot. Furthermore, by situating the reader within the fictional world of the book—perhaps in the surrogate role of protagonist or possibly in the voyeuristic role of eavesdropper (or, most likely, in both of these positions during the course of the reading)—Robbins is able to sustain his audience's interest in the experiences of a character who is in many ways other than sympathetic. On the one hand, Gwen Mati is snobbish, greedy, manipulative, and unpleasantly fastidious—she is, in fact, a person for whom Imelda Marcos is a model. On the other hand, about most things Gwen is a person of two minds, someone whose impulses are divided; and Robbins's second-person narrative voice is particularly well positioned to illustrate this for the reader. *Frog Pajamas*'s action focuses upon four days during which its protagonist's life dramatically changes. While specific events spark these changes, it is through the perspective offered by the narrative voice that readers are made aware of the ways in which Gwen Mati is, even when she does not realize it (or even when she actively resists it), already receptive to the changes spurred by the novel's plot.

PLOT DEVELOPMENT

On its most immediate level, *Frog Pajamas*'s plot takes the shape of a novelistic version of the classic Keystone comedy routine: its central action consists of a series of mad chases, comical misunderstandings, and other slapstick scenarios. The novel's linear sequence of events is divided into chapters that designate segments of time, "Thursday Night," "Friday Morning," etc., and these passages are further subdivided into the hours of the day. This method of structuring events serves to enhance the book's you-are-there effect; necessary background information about the characters is either provided by the narrator in speech addressed to the protagonist (and thus overheard by the reader) or revealed in characters' dialogue.

In the novel's opening scene, Gwen Mati is to be found commiserating with colleagues in the Bear & Bull, the bar that caters to members of Seattle's financial community. Naturally, the topic at hand is the dramatic market crash (the Dow Jones has dropped 873 points in a single day), and the assorted analysts, bankers, and brokers are waiting to learn how Japan's stock market will respond to news of the American disaster. Gwen, whose boss has broadly hinted that she might do well to consider another line of work, is not looking forward to a long weekend of worrying and wondering whether her career as broker is over. What she does not know, as she toys with her martinis, is that she is about to set forth on a series of adventures that will leave her little time to dwell on her impending misfortune. Before Monday morning dawns, Gwen will make five separate trips to the grocery store to purchase banana-flavored Popsicles. She will attend a meeting of herpetologists deeply concerned about a sharp decline in the earth's sundry frog populations, and she will gaze at Sirius A, the Dog Star, hoping to catch sight of Sirius B, the white dwarf that is its neighbor. Needless to say, pursuits such as these are well outside the range of the prim and socially self-conscious Gwen's ordinary occupations: they are among "the other oddities" that will seem to her to suddenly afflict her otherwise "orderly life" (120).

Three other characters play telling roles in Gwen's weekend of shenanigans, and she first meets one of these, Larry Diamond, while she is drinking in the Bear & Bull. Once an extraordinarily successful equity broker, Larry grew tired of playing his money games and therefore set himself up to take a fall in the crash of 1987. Having decided that "joy's always more important than juice ["jumbo juice" is the brokers' jargon for big money]" (191), Larry set out to have his "brain redone. A little cognitive redecorating" (182). He accomplished this by journeying to the ends of the earth—to Timbuktu, to be precise—and he plans to return to that distant city early on Monday morning. In the meantime, Larry is seeking an opportunity to meet with Dr. Yamaguchi, a cancer specialist who is visiting Seattle. At his clinic in Japan Dr. Yamaguchi has enjoyed remarkable success in curing colon cancer; Larry hopes that the doctor's technique might also work on his own case of rectal cancer. (From a different perspective, Gwen is also interested in Dr. Yamaguchi's successes. It turns out to be a faith in the market value of his therapy that forestalls the crash of the Nikkei, Japan's stock exchange.)

With the introduction of the other two characters central to its action, Robbins is ready to set *Frog Pajamas*'s picaresque plot in motion. Belford Dunn, a real estate agent, is Gwen's "annoying supposed boyfriend" (4). An overly earnest and deeply religious young man, one who constantly worries about the unfortunate plight of the homeless, Belford plans to leave his lucrative business and retrain to be a social worker. When he telephones Gwen at the Bear & Bull, it is to inform her that André, his pet Barbary ape, has escaped from his apartment. (Here Robbins returns to the theme of the pet monkey earlier introduced in *Another Roadside Attraction*.)

To assist Belford in his search for André, Gwen enlists the services of Q-Jo Huffington, the 300-pound tarot reader who is her neighbor and "supposed" friend. In addition to being one of Seattle's finest psychics, Q-Jo runs an extraordinary second business. For a small fee, she visits the homes of people who have gone on short excursions or taken extensive trips. She admires these travelers' scrapbooks and mementos and listens to their accounts of the wonders they have seen. In this way Q-Jo usefully serves as attentive audience for lonely people or for those who do not wish to bore acquaintances with a showing of the slides taken on their vacations.

Belford is understandably concerned about his pet's whereabouts because André is a "born-again" monkey. Trained by his original owner to participate in jewel heists, the animal was actually sentenced to die before Belford bribed French officials to secure his release. When Thursday night's efforts to locate the wayward ape prove to be fruitless, Belford begins to panic. He is fearful that without the prayer sessions to which he has become accustomed, André might be tempted to fall back into his old criminal ways. When it further occurs to him that the monkey's original owner might have been released from prison, and indeed might have arranged to somehow kidnap André, Belford determines that he must fly to San Francisco to consult with the French consul general.

Gwen is left to search for André, and on Good Friday it begins to become apparent to her that she must also search for Q-Jo, who seems to have vanished completely. Having once visited the Seattle police department to report a missing monkey, Gwen finds herself returning to report a missing person. (Through clever manipulation of his plot, Robbins mischievously arranges to repeatedly place Gwen in circumstances where she appears ridiculous to others.) Gwen's pursuit of Q-Jo leads her back to Larry Diamond, from whose apartment the psychic seems to have suddenly disappeared. As Larry explains the mysterious circumstances, he and Q-Jo were viewing slides of Timbuktu when he excused himself to visit the bathroom. When he returned some minutes later, Q-Jo was gone.

Gwen is in a quandary: is Larry Diamond what he appears to be— someone given to "pseudo-philosophical, nugatory babble" (98), someone who holds strange theories about the disappearance of the planet's frogs? Or is he some sort of vicious fiend who has murdered her friend Q-Jo? Perhaps he is the so-called Safe-Sex Rapist (a condom-wearing rapist), who has been haunting Seattle's neighborhoods. If, however, Larry is as harmless as he seems to be, he might be willing to help Gwen think of a way to salvage her career. With mixed feelings, Gwen decides to keep her options open. She therefore enlists Larry's assistance in her search for her missing friend.

Gwen sets forth on her quests to locate André and Q-Jo and to answer the puzzle of Larry Diamond with decidedly mixed motives. If she can find André, perhaps Belford will lend her the money she needs to try to reclaim her job. If that is not possible, and she finds that her career is over, then perhaps she will decide to marry Belford in an effort to preserve her costly standard of living. In either case, it seems worthwhile to her to launch a search for André, and she therefore invests in large quantities of banana Popsicles, the monkey's favorite treat. Gwen's attempts to entice André to visit her apartment prove to be successful, and thus at least one of her weekend's goals is satisfactorily achieved.

Gwen's wish to locate Q-Jo also arises, at least in part, out of her own pressing self-interests. Q-Jo has promised to give Gwen a tarot reading, and in the light of her uncertain future, Gwen is exceedingly eager to learn what it is that her cards might hold. In recent readings Gwen has selected the card that pictures the Fool, and Q-Jo has suggested that this

card signifies for her a journey out into the wondrous "world of experience" (91). Gwen, of course, feels that she is already undergoing this
promised journey, and she wishes to discuss it with her friend. She is,
therefore, left vacillating between feelings of anger and concern; Gwen
is annoyed that Q-Jo has apparently deserted her, and at the same time
she is concerned about her welfare. Torn by her conflicting emotions and
worried about her own destiny, Gwen dashes about Seattle trying to find
some order in a world that has, since Thursday, seemed to have become
increasingly confusing. A sense of order remains elusive, however, and
Gwen's confusion only deepens when she discovers that she is beginning
to find herself attracted to Larry Diamond.

As suggested by her tarot readings, Gwen's frantic comings and goings
over the Easter weekend constitute a journey into the world of experience. While *Frog Pajamas*'s protagonist thinks of her activities as efforts
to promote her immediate personal goals, the novel's design makes clear
that this character is actually engaged on a quest for an enlarged sense
of her own identity—an identity that has by chance and circumstance
been abruptly called into question. At this level of the novel's meaning,
its plot explores the psychology of a figure who is undergoing change.
Although she is at first reluctant to admit it, the market crash has indeed
brought an end to the life that Gwen has methodically fashioned for
herself, and she must therefore look into the bag that the Fool carries
over his shoulder to discover there the tools she needs to carry on with
her life's journey.

In the course of her Fool's journey, Gwen is often made to seem the
fool, to in some sense suffer the consequences of her own greedy and
selfish behavior—to experience a comeuppance. In the most dramatic of
these scenarios, she is assaulted by the Rich Boys, a gang of wealthy
hooligans whose favored pastime is tormenting the wandering homeless
and then speeding away in their expensive cars. Gwen is not physically
injured during these boys' malicious attack, but her sense of dignity is
shattered. The prim and proper young woman suffers the ignominy of
finding herself lying in Seattle's public streets bereft of her skirt and
panties. (The occurrence of other occasions upon which Gwen is shown
to appear in an awkward position suggests that the reader regard this
episode as a figurative as well as a literal de-pantsing.)

Although Gwen undeniably undergoes the experience of comeuppance, her quest is by no means simply an exercising of her own folly.
During the course of her long weekend she enjoys a sexual awakening
by finally opening herself to a relationship with Larry Diamond. She also

tells her father that she loves him, something she has not admitted for many, many years. Gwen's curious adventures have shown her a way to "lighten up," and when she finds that levity is one of the tools in the Fool's bag she carries, she begins to feel a freedom to express the various whims that she has through long course of habit firmly repressed. It is out of this newfound sense of freedom that Gwen concocts a bold and ingenious plan, a plan that turns out to be the brainchild of an outlaw.

As *Frog Pajamas* nears its climax, Gwen begins to narrow her options. On Easter Sunday Larry Diamond offers her a choice: either she can accept his gift of a one-way ticket to Timbuktu or she can choose another alternative, a set of notes in which Larry has outlined a plan whereby it might be possible for her to recoup her financial losses. Surprising herself by selecting the ticket, Gwen realizes that in making this choice she has effectively ended her career as broker—and thus also forfeited her chance of achieving her American dream. *Frog Pajamas*'s protagonist, however, is not quite ready to completely let go of the materialist side of her nature, and the novel therefore concludes with yet further shenanigans.

Making use of André's specialized skills, Gwen procures the jade enema nozzle that is essential to Dr. Yamaguchi's unusual cancer treatment. This is her gift to Larry (she knows that he will return it to the doctor after he has used it). Thinking in this instance about the welfare of another, Gwen performs with her outlaw's gesture an uncharacteristically selfless act. As for herself, she plans to make off with the Vincent Van Gogh drawing that hangs on Larry's neighbor's wall. With the money the drawing will bring, she can envision for herself a fine future in the Philippines as the "new Imelda Marcos" (385). However, when André finally emerges from the apartment he has burglarized, the object he is bearing is not the Van Gogh drawing: instead it is a tarot card, the card of the Fool. As Gwen ruefully studies her trophy, she notices that a message has been scribbled in its corner. The handwriting is unmistakably Q-Jo's, and what she has written is, "See you in Timbuktu!" (386).

CHARACTERS

In some respects *Frog Pajamas*'s protagonist can be compared with Sissy Hankshaw, for Gwen Mati strongly feels that she was born with certain disadvantages. Unlike Sissy, however, who accepts her condition and then finds a self-fulfilling way to transform her handicap into advantage, Gwen resentfully regrets what she regards as her marginal position within mainstream American society. Gwen's Filipino father is a bohemian musician, a jive-talking, marijuana-smoking throwback to the 1960s. Her Welsh mother, a poet and an admirer of Sylvia Plath, committed suicide when Gwen was still a child. Although the memory of her mother continues to haunt her, Gwen has purposefully chosen to fashion for herself a life that is in all possible ways different from that of her parents. Because she was not born to be the all-American girl, Gwen has determined that she will spare no effort in her endeavor to achieve that status on her own.

Gwen works very hard at the task of making herself into the person she wishes to appear to be. She once spent hours, for example, rerecording the message on her telephone answering machine before she felt that she had finally got it right. She does not like her voice, which is high, sweet, and bright (her father calls her Squeak). Believing that a throaty register would be more appropriate for a professional woman, she has tried drinking whiskey and smoking cigarettes in futile attempts to lower her voice. Gwen's methodical modeling of herself requires that she repress certain features of her personality. The reader is well aware of this, because in relating to the main character her deepest thoughts, the narrator exposes aspects of Gwen's identity that she generally keeps well hidden from others: her sharp eye for irony, for example, or her repressed sense of fun. (When Larry catches a rare glimpse of Gwen's fun-loving humor, he makes a comment about it. Gwen responds by explaining that she has been "a little out of control lately. . . . But," she hastens to assure him, "that's not who I am." Larry's reply is apt: "Who are you, Gwendolyn?" [277] he asks.)

About most things, and certainly about the people in her life, Gwen is distinctly a person of two minds. It is by portraying her character in this light that the writer shows her to be someone whose sense of identity is in a state of flux, someone who cannot, it seems, truly make up her mind. Gwen is obviously ambivalent about Belford Dunn, the man the narrator refers to as "your annoying supposed boyfriend" (4). Although she thinks she looks forward to the day when she can leave him behind, when *Frog Pajamas*'s action opens, Gwen has already been seeing Belford for more than three years. Moreover, when he travels to San Francisco, she acknowledges to herself that she misses having him around. Gwen is also of two minds about her "supposed" friend Q-Jo Huffington. On the one hand, she is embarrassed to be seen in public with the "baggy flake" who sports bright turbans and swirling caftans, but, "privately," she has "always found Q-Jo's size appealing," (24) a source of stability and comfort. Of course Gwen is also drawn to her psychic friend because Q-Jo is able to tell her interesting things about herself—things of which Gwen has not always been aware as well as things that she does not necessarily accept. In this respect Q-Jo resembles the narrator, for she clearly sees a side of Gwen that remains invisible to others.

Within the context of *Frog Pajamas*'s most significant theme, Gwen Mati serves as the embodiment of the materialistic impulse. She is a person who has come to believe that it is through possessing things that she can establish her own worth. For instance, Gwen has signed a contract to purchase a fancy condominium with a view of Puget Sound. In her system of measuring value, it is by dint of possessing this desirable view (actually enjoying it is incidental) that she can demonstrate to herself and others that she is moving upward in the world. For Gwen, the possession of a new address will signify that she has risen well above the social sphere of her old friends, and she therefore plans to use the occasion of its acquisition to cut off her relations with Belford and Q-Jo. Because so much of Gwen's sense of her own selfhood has come to rest upon her material position, it is little wonder that the market crash depicted in the book has had the effect of casting her into a crisis of identity.

In readily apparent ways, *Frog Pajamas*'s other significant characters serve as foils to the protagonist whose life is so dramatically laid open by the novel's narrative technique. The various purposes that are represented in the figures of Belford, Larry, and Q-Jo stand in sharp contrast to Gwen's narrow, materialist ambitions. From their different perspectives, all of these other characters are interested in a world that extends well beyond the physical boundaries of the self. While it is obvious that it is out of her emotional defenses (in great part, out of her terrible grief over her mother's death) that Gwen has turned her attention inward and sought to find security by defining herself through what she owns, the other characters perceive reality in terms that are very different from Gwen's.

In his sympathy for the homeless, Belford is concerned about an immediate reality in which human suffering occurs. Larry, who has experienced much suffering himself (first autism and then cancer), realizes that everyone has a hard-luck story for the telling. It is not these individual stories that capture his attention, but a different kind of story, one that has implications for the collective human race. He is concerned about a cosmic reality, one in which people's destiny can be understood in relation to that of the universe itself. His account of the Bozo and

Dogon theories of a cosmic connection to Sirius, the Dog Star, is naturally of interest to Q-Jo, who as a psychic is centrally concerned with spiritual realities. The woman who listens to the stories of people's journeys regards life as a grand journey, an adventure, and a quest. (The inexplicable fact of Q-Jo's sudden and mysterious disappearance hints that she has set forth on some marvelous quest of her own.)

When Q-Jo describes for Gwen the kinds of experiences that characterize the Fool's life journey, she remarks upon the tempters and the teachers that the Fool is likely to encounter. At the level of the novel's meaning that portrays Gwen's life as quest, *Frog Pajamas*'s secondary characters play out these roles in their relations to the protagonist. Although Gwen might regard Larry Diamond as a tempter, someone who seeks to divert her from the course she has determinedly plotted for herself, in truth he plays the role of teacher, the part of the sage who possesses surprising bits of wisdom (including an ability to communicate through telepathy). In this respect Larry closely resembles the Chink, The Woodpecker, and Wiggs Dannyboy, characters who broaden the horizons of *Cowgirls*'s Sissy Hankshaw, *Still Life*'s Princess Leigh-Cheri, and *Jitterbug Perfume*'s Priscilla Partido. Like these other figures, Larry is the outlaw/philosopher, the man who lives his life apart from society's norms and institutions. He desires to show Gwen that the world can offer her much more than the seductive money games she plays.

As Gwen's self-appointed spiritual counselor, Q-Jo is clearly another of her teachers. A character greatly admired by *Frog Pajamas*'s reviewers (several of whom express regret that she disappears so quickly), Q-Jo appears to be the very person that Gwen obviously is not, a kind of shadow self of the protagonist. Q-Jo is ebullient where Gwen is restrained, she is sensuous where Gwen is puritanically repressed, and she is intuitively sensitive to the positions of others where Gwen remains oblivious to what other people think. Whereas Gwen has completely devoted herself to the material world, Q-Jo spends much of her time on the astral plane; it is her purpose to try to persuade Gwen that she too possesses a spiritual dimension.

If Belford appears to be a most unlikely kind of tempter, he nevertheless plays that role in Gwendolyn's experiences. Belford is a thoroughly predictable—and dull—young man, one who does not truly interest Gwen, one whose unchanging relationship to her seems merely safe. For *Frog Pajamas*'s protagonist, he represents an easy escape from her dilemma: should Gwen choose a marriage of convenience, then her decision will mean that she must continue to repress the spiritual side of her nature in favor of her obsessive desire for the security she associates with a material reality. Tellingly, it is when Gwen hangs up on Belford, who has called from San Francisco, that she first experiences a feeling of freedom and release. At that moment, she realizes that "something has changed. You have changed. . . . and you may never be the same" (122). It is when she turns away from the temptation represented by Belford that Gwen finds herself ready to engage a wholly new world of experience.

STYLE

Reviewers of Robbins's books at times express noticeable differences of opinion about the nature of his subject matter or about the relative success of his invariably interesting experiments with narrative technique. Differences such as these notwithstanding, there is nevertheless widespread agreement about this writer's virtuosity as stylist. Describing him as "a wonderfully original writer," reviewer Andy Solomon associates Robbins's energetic phrasing and elaborate conceits with the fanciful language of the baroque: as he says, "in contemporary fiction, only Lorrie Moore matches Robbins's early-Shakespearean delight in wordplay and extravagant imagery" (Solomon 6).

Robbins's striking observations, often expressed in "phrases of mind-boggling beauty" (Rucker 1), characteristically offer insights that go well beyond the merely descriptive. For example, in passages that characterize the qualities of Seattle's own special kind of rain, Robbins's narrator shows how it enfolds the objects in its path. Gwen's building "is surrounded by the soft, the gray, and the moist, as if it is being digested by an oyster" (114). As is the case with so many of her feelings, Gwen is of two different minds about the constant presence of the rain. On the one hand, she finds it protective—it "dampens the dragon's fire." But, on the other hand, "like the pockets of a drowned sailor, it can conceal disintegrating packets of forbidden opiates and any number of rusty knives" (115). Thus, in imagery startlingly rich and strange, imagery that suggests how the rain both comfortingly envelops and threateningly conceals, the writer uses a detail of the landscape to offer insight into his character's divided state of mind.

Two of Robbins's delightfully imaginative conceits embody themes central to his novel. In the course of her journey toward self-realization, Gwen Mati must learn the hard lesson that the life she has mapped out for herself is not one that truly suits her. Gwen has obviously constructed her identity out of her own emotional defenses. In doing this, as the novel makes clear, she has been reading her life's script from the "wrong libretto" (98). The libretto, as Robbins's metaphor suggests, offers an account of what is happening in the "theater of existence" (98). If the script is the wrong one, the person who is following it will likely misread the drama that unfolds. Extending his metaphor to embrace the society surrounding Gwen, Robbins notes that the librettos commonly provided by advertisers, politicians, or other representatives of social institutions can also prove to be "dangerously misleading" (98). In *Frog Pajamas*, the conceit of the wrong libretto serves a purpose similar to that of *Skinny Legs*'s metaphoric use of Salome's seven veils.

Robbins introduces a delicate and utterly charming conceit when Gwen hangs up on Belford and then immediately acknowledges that her life has suddenly been changed. At that moment she recalls an anecdote related by her father: Dizzy Gillespie, it seems, once bent his trumpet by sitting upon it. In doing this, he quite accidentally created the "instrument that transformed his career" (122). Change, it seems to Gwen, can occur in an instant, and when it does, "the next thing one knows, one is blowing a whole new tune" (122). From this point in the novel, Gwen is well aware that her "horn is tipped now ever so slightly toward the stars," and that there appears to be "a fresh melodic line" that she seems "destined to pursue" (127). Knowing that her trumpet is now bent, Gwen finds herself ready to set forth on her Fool's journey.

THEME

Above all, *Frog Pajamas* tells a rollicking story of greed and folly. As reviewer Robert H. Donahugh points out, Robbins has once again written "a very funny book that might incite a bit of thinking as well as laughter" (Donahugh 92). Admittedly interested in evoking in his readers both of these responses, Robbins tempers his sharply satiric critique of greed with his characteristically broad vision of human folly. In Robbins's peculiarly humane worldview, where his characters comprise a marvelously hilarious ship of fools, the laughter turns out to be at everyone's expense.

Greed, that most egocentric of human impulses, is shown within the novel's pages to lead to the kind of self-preoccupation that can severely restrict the range of experiences presented by the world. This is true both for those who have plenty but nonetheless find themselves greedy for more (Gwen Mati and the financial brokers) and for those who have nothing at all and find themselves greedy for something (the desperate panhandlers who accost passersby on the streets of Seattle). In both cases—one the result of a personal obsession and the other the result of an unwanted necessity—lives are limited because characters' attention is focused exclusively upon the material dimension of the world.

If the market crash of 1987 signaled a warning within the culture of greed that seems to have defined the 1980s, *Frog Pajamas* insists that the message implicit in that event remains pertinent during the 1990s. In its depictions of the homeless, Robbins's sixth novel presents a critique of the materialist society whose values promote the social injustices commonly experienced by people who are poor. For the homeless, insult is grievously added to injury when the Rich Boys, with nothing better to do, descend upon them to carry out their gratuitous assaults. The Rich Boys have clearly depersonalized the homeless, have chosen to regard them as figures without faces; but readers are reminded that the poor do indeed have faces when Gwen encounters among them a panhandler who used to be a teller in the bank that handles her account. In a society where the "schism between rich and poor" (41) appears to be growing, and where another market crash could effectively widen that schism, it is quite apparent that the playing of the money game has engendered vicious repercussions.

It is through his use of the second-person point of view that Robbins seeks to dramatize the role that a fascination for the material plays in contemporary American society. Because Gwen Mati is the character who is shown to embody the selfish desire for excess that exists within her culture and because the novel's world is envisioned in relation to her perspective, readers—who at times find themselves in sympathy with Gwen and at other times do not—are necessarily positioned to address for themselves the issue of greed that is raised by the novel. Just as Gwen is a product of the society in which she is a member, so too is the reader.

The subject of human folly is one of Robbins's persistent themes, and *Frog Pajamas* offers readers a veritable carnival of foolishness. In one way or another all of the novel's characters take on the role of fool, for in Robbins's comic vision human folly seems inevitable. Gwen, at first, actively resists the role of fool, but both Larry and Q-Jo possess the kind of wisdom that admits the necessity of risking folly, of sometimes choosing to act against the social grain. In describing a human life as a quest for understanding, Q-Jo points out to Gwen that "the only ones who'll ever reach that goal are the ones who have the courage to make fools of themselves along the way" (91).

Larry, Q-Jo, Dr. Yamaguchi, and finally Gwen herself (whose last act of folly requires the courage of the fool) all prove to be willing to make fools of themselves, but another kind of foolishness is also depicted within the novel's pages. Before she decides to set forth on her Fool's journey, Gwen in fact plays the part of the dupe—that is, the role of the unwitting fool. (It is in this guise that the protagonist appears to be served her just deserts.)

Clearly, Belford Dunn is another dupe, and one of the novel's most comical scenes depicts his utter foolishness (this scene is reminiscent of those in which Gwen is shown to be ridiculous). When Belford returns from San Francisco, he immediately heads for Gwen's apartment. The tableau that he finds there is one that brings tears of joy to his eyes: Gwen and André are sitting together reading from the Bible. In his assumption that a born-again Gwen has been communing with his born-again ape, Belford is, of course, completely mistaken. Gwen has happened to drag out her Bible simply because she wishes to check Larry Diamond's veracity (he has informed her that a superfluity of frogs was among the plagues visited upon ancient Egypt). *Frog Pajamas* delights in scenes such as this one, where the reader is made privy to the occasion of its characters' unwitting folly.

ALTERNATIVE READING: A MARXIST PERSPECTIVE

Rudy Rucker closes his review of *Half Asleep in Frog Pajamas* with a tribute to its author. "Rant on, Robbins," he says. "Our carking, swinking, workaday world needs you" (Rucker 1). Rucker's allusion to the workaday world is altogether apt, for Robbins has had much to say about that world within the pages of his novel. Because Karl Marx was also immensely interested in the subject of work, it seems appropriate to consider *Frog Pajamas*'s vision of the contemporary working world in the light of Marx's insights and perspective.

Karl Marx was a social and political philosopher who focused his attention upon the crucial importance of economics in human social arrangements. He argued, in fact, that a society's economic system—its modes of producing the means by which its people live—gives shape to that society, to its values, and to the experiences of its members. Marx greatly feared that in a capitalist society, such as the one portrayed in *Frog Pajamas*, the persistence of class distinctions inevitably operates to promote social injustice. He saw that the wealthy, who exercise control over the means of production, are obviously positioned to exploit the working class. Of course, in a capitalist economy where there is a large, influential, and well-rewarded middle class, the power of the wealthy class is necessarily much diminished. Ominously, however, in *Frog Pajamas*'s economic landscape the "schism" between the rich and the poor is shown to be widening—and when that is the case, the social stability provided by a shrinking middle class can begin to be threatened. It is in this context that Robbins's account of the predations of the Rich Boys serves as an allegorical reminder of the power of the rich to prey upon the poor.

Given that work is essential within human societies, Marx was deeply interested in the systems of value that are based upon labor. His critique of a capitalistic, industrial economy particularly addressed the troubling problem of alienation within the workplace. People, Marx believed, need to take satisfaction in their work and to fully share in the productivity that is the result of their labor. While these objectives are often attainable for members of the middle class, such is not the case for people in the working class, where labor is assigned little value. Thus Michael, the waiter whom Gwen snubs in the Bear & Bull, might well feel that the service he performs is not appreciated—or that its value is not worthy of notice. That Gwen knows his name but chooses not to use it demonstrates her desire to observe class distinctions. As was the case with his portrayal of the Daughters of the Daily Special, Robbins uses the example of restaurant service to depict the alienation of the working class.

While *Frog Pajamas* focuses its attention upon the threatened middle class (the class immediately endangered by the stock market collapse), it is interesting to consider the question of work in respect to two other classes depicted in the novel. Neither the Rich Boys, who are living the life of leisure provided by their capital, nor the homeless, who are dispossessed, enjoy the human satisfaction that is made available in work. The homeless, of course, are living their lives at the level of mere survival, but the aristocratic Rich Boys, whose survival is guaranteed, are using their leisure time to engage in nonproductive activity. Within Robbin's book, the kind of purpose that meaningful work can bring to a human life is not being realized in the experiences of the members of either of these classes.

For Gwen Mati, *Frog Pajamas*'s main representative of the working middle class, Marx's ideal of meaningful work is not even an issue. Tellingly, Robbins's protagonist always thinks of her work as her "job." Gwen has chosen her line of work not because she likes it (and it is absolutely clear that she is not good at it at all), but because she has completely subscribed to the social values defined by the greedy 1980s.[2] Gwen likes money, and she therefore likes the capitalist idea of making money out of money, but she does not think of her occupation as satisfying work. Like the jobs of many members of the working class, hers is merely a possible means to a seemingly necessary end, and she thus suffers alienation within her workplace. Her position can be contrasted with that of Q-Jo, who enjoys her work and believes that it is usefully productive, or with that of Belford, who is very good at what he does but has come to believe that a more socially responsible occupation would afford him greater satisfaction.

The distinction between work and a job is delineated in *Frog Pajamas* in an interesting conversation that Gwen Mati has with Larry Diamond. Larry observes that within the world's "social history, jobs are an aberration, a flash in the pan" (195). While people have always found it necessary to work, they have held jobs, Larry claims, for only a few hundred years. Pointing out that within a capitalist economy the "state uses jobs, or rather the illusion of jobs, as a mechanism for control" (196), Larry implicitly argues for a Marxist apprehension of the differences between satisfying, meaningful work and a job that serves only the purpose of gainful employment. When Gwen wonders if the people who are worried about jobs are perhaps reading from the "wrong libretto," Larry is delighted. Maybe "there's hope for you yet," (196) he exclaims.

(For additional insights into Marxist critical approaches, see chapter 6.)

NOTES

1. Butor's novel was entitled *La Modification* in the original French. The title has also been translated as *Second Thoughts*.

2. In portraying Gwen as a commodities broker, as a thoroughgoing capitalist in the purest sense of the term, Robbins sharpens his critique of America's culture of greed. A devout worshiper of the false god of money, Gwen begins each day with a moment of meditation: her morning mantra consists of a complete recitation of the names of the companies that make up the Dow Jones Industrials.

Bibliography

WORKS

Novels by Tom Robbins

Another Roadside Attraction. 1971. New York: Bantam, 1990.
Even Cowgirls Get the Blues. New York: Houghton Mifflin, April 1976. Serialized in *High Times,* June 1976.
Guy Anderson. Gear Works Press, 1965.
Half Asleep in Frog Pajamas. New York: Bantam, 1994.
Jitterbug Perfume. New York: Bantam, 1984.
Skinny Legs and All. New York: Bantam, 1990.
Still Life with Woodpecker: A Sort of a Love Story. New York: Bantam, 1980.

Articles

"Atlantis Is Rising." *Helix* 5, 3 (31 October 1968): 12–13.
"Confessions of a Reluctant Sex Goddess." *Esquire,* February 1993: 70–76.
"The Day the Earth Spit Wart Hogs." *Esquire,* Winter Traveler, October 1985: 1[+].
"Feminismo." [Sometimes reprinted as "Move Over Macho, Here Comes Feminismo," originally published in *Seattle Weekly* as "Notes on Nukes..."]
"The Genius Waitress: An Ode to Women Who Serve." *Playboy,* December 1991: 144–45.

"The Hair of the Beast." *Esquire*, November 1984: 236–38⁺.

"Hendrix." *Helix* 3, 1 (15 February 1968): 2.

"The Kiss." *Playboy*, February 1990: 92–93.

"Imagination." *Self*, May 1994: 230.

Letter to the author, 15 March 1995.

Letter to the author, 26 June 1995.

Letter to the author, 28 July 1995.

"Mini, a Natural High." *New York Times*, 6 April 1995: C1⁺.

"My Life with Picasso." *Helix* 11, 5 (29 January 1970): 10.

"Nadia Salerno-Sonnenberg." *Esquire*, November 1989: 172–73.

"Notes from the Underground." *Helix*, n.d.: 9.

"Notes on Nukes, Nookie, and Neo-Romanticism." *The Weekly: Seattle's News-Magazine*, 21–27 June 1978: 11–15. [Plus: Letters and response from Tom Robbins in *The Weekly*: Seattle's News-Magazine, 19–25 July 1978: 5–6.]

Personal Interview, 24 August 1994.

Personal Interview, 14 March 1995.

"Obituary." *Utne Reader*, September/October 1988: 97–99.

"Ode to Redheads." *Gentlemen's Quarterly*, June 1988: 216–19.

"The Purpose of the Moon." *Playboy*, January 1979: 237, 330.

"Ray Kroc Did It All for You." *Esquire*, December 1983: 340–42⁺.

"The Real Valley of the Dolls (Shoshoni Rock Drawings in Nevada's North Canyon)." *Esquire*, December 1988: 202–6⁺.

Robbins, Tom et al. "And We Bid You Good Night." *Rolling Stone*, 21 September 1995: 30⁺.

"Skinny Legs and All." *Esquire*, April 1990: 149–60.

"This Is the END." *Helix* 1, 8 (25 July 1967): 1.

"Tom Robbins Considers the Man in the Tower." Booklet/various artists *Tower of Song: The Songs of Leonard Cohen*, CD, A & M Records, 1995.

Tom Robbins, The Visual Arts, 1963–1964. Seattle: J. Dille, 1985.

"Treasured Places." *Life*, July 1987: 35–42⁺.

"Two in the Bush (Okavango Delta)." *Esquire*, March 1990: 50⁺.

"Wishing for Milton's Power & Tolstoy's Zaniness." *New York Times Book Review* 90 (8 December 1985): 46–47.

"Women We Love." *Esquire*, August 1992: 78–92.

"Writing and Politics." *Fiction International* 15, 1 (1984): 24.

"Writing from the Inside Out: Style Is Not the Frosting; It's the Cake." Lecture, Yale University, 6 October 1994.

"Yet Another Roadside Attraction (Ruby Montana's Pinto Pony Collectibles Shop)." *House & Garden*, August 1991: 38⁺.

"You Gotta Have Soul." *Esquire*, October 1993: 120.

MEDIA APPEARANCES BY OR ADAPTATIONS OF TOM ROBBINS

Cott, Jonathan. "Drugstore Cowgirl." *Rolling Stone*, 11 November 1993: 58–62.
"Don't Fence Him In." *Chicago Tribune*, 15 May 1994: 13, 16.
Even Cowgirls Get the Blues. 1994. Director: Gus Van Sant.
Hansen, Liane. "Novelist Tom Robbins Loves to Play with Language." *National Public Radio Sunday Weekend Edition*, 4 September 1994. Program 1087.
Made in Heaven. 1987. Director: Alan Rudolph.
Mrs. Parker and the Vicious Circle. 1994. Director: Alan Rudolph.
Robbins, Tom. *1994 Country Music Awards* appearance, MTV.
——. Radio programs on WKRAB on Sundays (1967). (See advertisement for programs in *Helix* 1, 4 [16 May 1967]: 10.)
——. *Seattle Times* articles. (See "Articles by Tom Robbins—*The Visual Arts*" list.)
——. The Tom Robbins Homepage. http://www.rain.org/~da5e/tom_robbins.html.
——. Usenet newsgroup (alt.fan.tom-robbins). Mailing list: MAGIC-L. Mail to: listserv@American.edu.

ARTICLES AND MONOGRAPHS ABOUT TOM ROBBINS

Batchelor, John Calvin. "Package of the Artist as a Young Seer." *Soho Weekly News*, 13 January 1977.
Christy, George. "Tom Robbins." *Interview*, November 1993: 126–31.
Coburn, Randy Sue. "Tom Robbins, the Storyteller Who Lives in a Tree." *Washington Star*, 20 June 1976, Calendar sec., 1, 25.
Dialogues with Northwest Writers. Northwest Review of Books, 1982: 95–102.
Edlin, Mari. "Tom Robbins." *Publishers Weekly*, 25 May 1990: 41–42.
Egan, Peter. "Writers Remember: American Authors Look Back on Their Cars." *Road & Track*, January 1987: 108+.
Egan, Timothy. "Blue Moon Tavern." *Seattle Access*. New York: Access Press, 1993: 185.
——. "Perfect Sentences, Imperfect Universe." *New York Times*, 30 December 1993, late ed.: C1+.
Fry, Donn. "Robbins' Latest Trip Takes His Readers to Timbuktu." *Seattle Times* and *Post Intelligencer*, "Arts Alive," 21 August 1994: M 1–4.
Gerson, Steven M. "Return with Us Now to Those Thrilling Days of Yesteryear: The Sixties in Robbins' *Even Cowgirls Get the Blues*." *McNeese Review* 28 (1981–82): 73–82.
Gottschall, Claudia. " 'Unspeakable Visions': Beat Consciousness and Its Textual Representation." *DAI* 54, 9 (March 1994): 3435A–36A.

Gross, Beverly. "Misfits: Tom Robbins' *Even Cowgirls Get the Blues.*" *North Dakota Quarterly* 50, 3 (Summer 1982): 36–51.

Horowitz, M. G. "Cosmic Partners: On the Central Oregon Set of *Even Cowgirls Get the Blues* with Co-Conspirators Tom Robbins & Gus Van Sant." *Pacific Northwest,* 1 July 1993: 38–41.

Howell, Pamela Rene. "Reality as Fabulous: Fantasy as Rhetorical Imperative in the Contemporary American Novel." *DAI* 44, 8 (February 1984): 2472A–73A.

Jenks, Tom. "How Writers Live Today." *Esquire,* August 1985: 123–27.

Karl, Frederick R. "Growing Up in America: The 1940's and Thereafter." *American Fictions, 1940/1980: A Comprehensive History and Critical Evaluations.* New York: Harper & Row, 1983: 129–75.

Klinkowitz, Jerome, and Loree Rackstraw. "The American 1970's: Recent Intellectual Trends." *Review Française d'Etudes Américaines* 8 (1979): 243–54.

McCaffery, Larry, and Sinda Gregory, eds. "Tom Robbins." Interview in *Alive and Writing: Interviews with American Authors of the 1980's.* Urbana: University of Illinois Press, 1987: 222–39.

Matera, Mariane. "Bohemian Rhapsody." *Livewire,* 1 October 1992: 9.

Maxwell, Jessica. "Tom Robbins's Book of Bozo." *Esquire,* January 1995: 18+. (Interview.)

Miller, Patricia Cleary. "Reconciling Science and Mysticism: Characterization in the Novels of Tom Robbins." *DAI* 40 (1979): 2666H.

Mitchell, Greg. ". . . And *Cowgirls* Jumped Over the Moon." *Crawdaddy,* August 1977: 29–33.

Nadeau, Robert. "Physics and Cosmology in the Fiction of Tom Robbins." *Critique: Studies in Modern Fiction* 20 (1978): 63–74.

Nathan, Paul S. "Rights and Permissions." *Publishers Weekly,* 4 April 1977: 52.

Nelson, William. "The Comic Grotesque in Recent Fiction." *Thalia: Studies in Literary Humor* 5, 2 (Fall/Winter 1982–83): 36–40.

———. "Unlikely Heroes: The Central Figures in *The World According to Garp, Even Cowgirls Get the Blues,* and *A Confederacy of Dunces.*" In *The Hero in Transition,* edited by Ray B. Browne and Marshall W. Fishwick. Bowling Green, Ohio: Bowling Green University Popular Press, 1983: 163–70.

O'Connell, Nicholas. *At the Field's End: Interviews with 20 Pacific Northwest Writers.* Seattle: Madrona Publishers, 1987: 264–84.

Portela, María Alejandra. "John Barth, Thomas McGuane y Tom Robbins: *A Lo Largo de la Pluralidad Whitmaniana,*" edited by Rolando Costa Picazo. In *Estados Unidos y America Latina: Relaciones Interculturales,* Buenos Aires: Asociation Argentina de Estudios Americans, 1994: 221–29.

Puhr, K. M. "Postmodernism for High-School Students." *English Journal* 81 (January 1992): 64–67.

Robbins, Tom. *Current Biography Yearbook.* New York: Wilson, 1993: 493–97.

Rogers, Michael. "Taking Tom Robins Seriously." *Rolling Stone*, 17 November 1977: 66–71.

Ross, Mitchell S. "Prince of the Paperback Literati." *New York Times Magazine*, 12 February 1978: 16–17, 66–69, 72–77, 86.

Siegel, Mark. "The Meaning of Meaning in the Novels of Tom Robbins." *Mosaic* 14, 3 (Summer 1981): 119–31.

Siegel, Mark Richard. *Tom Robbins*. Idaho: Boise State University Press, 1980.

Skagit Valley Writers' League. *Authors of Skagit County, 1883–1983*. Pacific Northwest Publishing, 1983.

Strelow, Michael. "Dialogue with Tom Robbins." *Northwest Review* 20, 2/3 (1982): 97–102.

"Tom Robbins." *Contemporary Literary Criticism*. Vol. 64. Detroit: Gale Research, 1991: 370–85.

"Tom Robbins." *Current Biography* 54, 6 (June 1993): 44–49.

Tonnelli, Bill. "Tom Robbins: The Spirit of the Letter." *Esquire*, June 1996: 68–69.

Venn, George. "Continuity in Northwest Literature." In *NW Perspectives: Essays on the Culture of the Pacific NW*, edited by Edwin R. Bingham and Glen A. Love. Seattle: University of Washington Press, 1979: 98–118.

Wheeler, Elizabeth Patricia. "The Frontier Sensibility in Novels of Jack Kerouac, Richard Brautigan and Tom Robbins." *DAI* 46, 4 (October 1985): 985A.

Wilson, Raymond. "A Synthesis of Modernism." *Prairie Schooner* 51 (Spring 1977): 99–100.

REVIEWS AND CRITICISM

Another Roadside Attraction

Book List, 15 September 1971: 84.

Books & Bookmen, July 1973: 112.

Kirkus Review, 11 March 1971: 256.

Library Journal, 15 May 1971: 1729.

National Review, 19 January 1973: 103.

New Republic, 26 January 1971. 29.

Observer (London), 8 April 1973: 37.

Publishers Weekly, 22 February 1971: 139.

Publishers Weekly, 19 January 1972: 61.

Sharlin, Shifra. "Square and Groovy Gods Made Flesh." *Books & Religion* 17 (Fall 1990): 5, 6, 14.

Toomajian, Janice. *Voice of Youth Advocates*, August 1981: 47.

Washington Post Book World, 21 September 1980: 12.
Waugh, Auberon. "Butterfly Nut." *Spectator*, 24 March 1973: 365–66.

Even Cowgirls Get the Blues

Baker, William. *Antioch Review* 35 (Fall 1977): 458.
Le Clair, Thomas. *New York Times Book Review*, 3 April 1977: 52.
Nathan, Paul S. "Border Crossing." *Publishers Weekly*, 4 April 1977: 52.
Publishers Weekly, 14 February 1977: 82.
Rogers, Michael. "Taking Tom Robbins Seriously." *Rolling Stone*, 17 November 1977: 66–71.
School Library Journal, October 1983: 132.
Treglown, Jeremy. *New Statesman*, 12 August 1977: 219–20.
Wilson, Raymond J., III. *Prairie Schooner*, Spring 1977: 99–100.

Jitterbug Perfume

Analog 105 (August 1985): 178.
Book List, 1 October 1984: 147.
Delacorte, Peter. "A Search for Immortality." *San Francisco Chronicle*, 25 November 1984, sec. 3: 1.
Dougherty, Steven. "Cowgirls May Get the Blues, but Not Tom Robbins, Who Pours It On in *Jitterbug Perfume*." *People Weekly*, 1 April 1985: 123–24+.
House, John. "They Brake for Unicorns." *New York Times Book Review*, 9 December 1984, sec. 7: 11.
Kirkus Review, January 1984: 927.
KJG. *West Coast Review of Books*, March 1985: 31.
Library Journal, January 1985: 102.
Los Angeles Times Book Review, 16 December 1984: 37.
New Yorker, 7 January 1985: 78.
Pautz, Peter D. "The Beet, Noblest of Vegetables." *Fantasy Review* 8 (February 1985): 20.
Publishers Weekly, December 1984: 40.
Publishers Weekly, April 1985: 75.
Ross, Mitchell S. "Jitterbug Perfume." *National Review*, 28 June 1985: 44–45.
Rucker, Rudy. "In Search of the Ultimate Love Potion." *Washington Post Book World*, 25 November 1984: 1.
San Francisco Chronicle, 6 July 1985: 45.
Whitmer, Peter O. "Cosmic Comedian." *Saturday Review*, January/February 1985: 50–55.

Still Life with Woodpecker

American Book Review, March 1981: 14.

Best Sellers 40 (November 1980): 275.

Book List 77 (1 September 1980): 5.

Cassill, R. V. *New York Times Book Review*, 28 September 1980: 15.

Clark, Jeff. *Library Journal*, 19 January 1980: 2108.

Finkle, David. *Village Voice*, 5 November 1980: 46.

Flannery, Susan. *School Library Journal* 27 (January 1981): 1975.

Geringer, Laura. *Newsweek*, 29 September 1980: 82.

Halpern, S. M. *Nation*, 5 February 1980: 415.

Kirkus Review, 15 July 1980: 935.

Lownsbrough, John. "A Shot of Tequila, a Dose of Whimsy." *Maclean*, June 1980: 63.

McConnell, Frank. *Commonwealth*, 13 March 1981: 153.

Norman, Peter. *Times Literary Supplement*, 1 March 1980: 1220.

Peters, Julie B. *Saturday Review*, September 1980: 71–72.

Publishers Weekly, 25 July 1980: 155.

Washington Post Book World, 28 September 1980: 5.

Skinny Legs and All

Aiello, John. "The Same Old Road for Tom Robbins." *San Francisco Chronicle*, 12 April 1990: E5.

Balzar, John. "Writer Tom Robbins: A Man of La Conner." *Los Angeles Times*, 6 April 1990: E1.

Book List 86 (15 January 1990): 954.

Cantor, Jay. "Yet Another Roadside Attraction." *Washington Post Book World*, 25 March 1990: 1, 9.

Clark, Tom. "Through Salome's Veils to Ultimate Cognition." *Los Angeles Times Book Review*, 15 April 1990: 1, 9.

Dickinson, Charles. "Playful Absurdities." *Chicago Tribune—Books*, 1 April 1990: 3.

Eckhoff, Sally S. *Village Voice Literary Supplement*, June 1990: 6.

Kirkus Review, 15 February 1990: 216.

Lemon, Lee. "Skinny Legs and All." *Prairie Schooner*, Winter 1990: 129–31.

Locus 25 (July 1990): 60.

Locus 25 (November 1990): 60.

Locus 26 (May 1991): 49.

Los Angeles Times Book Review, 24 March 1991: 10.

Queenan, Joe. "Then the Spoon Speaks Up." *New York Times Book Review*, 15 April 1990: 12.

Rungren, Lawrence. "Skinny Legs and All." *Library Journal*, 1 March 1990: 117.

Skow, John. "Skinny Legs and All." *Time*, 7 May 1990: 112.

Steinberg, Sybil. "Skinny Legs and All." *Publishers Weekly*, 16 February 1990: 68.

Wall Street Journal, 23 March 1990: A13.

Half Asleep in Frog Pajamas

Campbell, Susan. " 'Half Asleep': An Experience for the Psyche." *Hartford Courant*, 4 September 1994.

Curwen, Thomas. "Half Asleep in Frog Pajamas." *People Weekly*, 16 January 1995: 31+.

Donahugh, Robert H. "Half Asleep in Frog Pajamas." *Library Journal*, 15 September 1994: 92.

Elbling, Peter. "Just an Old-fashioned Love Song." *Los Angeles Times Book Review*, 25 September 1994: 1.

Hooper, Brad. "Upfront Fall Review: Adult Fiction." *Book List* 90 (22 August 1994): 1992.

Karbo, Karen. "The Ocean's Zither." *New York Times Book Review*, 30 October 1994: 27.

Maryles, Daisy. "A Dynamic Duo." *Publishers Weekly*, 12 September 1994: 16.

Milligan, Peter. "Tome Invasion." *Melody Maker*, 72, 12 (25 March 1995): 15.

"Pajama Promotion." *Publishers Weekly*, 21 November 1994.

Petrakos, Chris. "Tom Robbins's Latest Overdoes the Quirkiness." *Chicago Tribune*, 17 November 1994: 5.

Publishers Weekly, 15 August 1994: 86.

Rucker, Rudy. "The Transcendent Wisdom of Amphibians." *Washington Post Book World*, 18 December 1994: 1.

Solomon, Andy. "Robbins Looks Good in Frog Pajamas." *San Francisco Chronicle*, 6 September 1994, sec. 6: 6.

WORKS OF GENERAL INTEREST

Atwood, Margaret. *Good Bones and Simple Murders*. New York: Bantam Doubleday, 1994.

Bettelheim, Bruno. *The Uses of Enchantment: The Power and Importance of Fairy Tales*. Harmondsworth: Penguin, 1978.

Booth, Wayne. *The Rhetoric of Fiction*. Chicago: University of Chicago Press, 1961.

Broumas, Olga. *Beginning with "O."* New Haven, CT: Yale University Press, 1977.

Campbell, Joseph. *The Hero with a Thousand Faces*. Princeton, N.J.: Princeton University Press, 1949.

———. *The Masks of God: Creative Mythology*. New York: Viking Press, 1968.

———. *The Masks of God: Occidental Mythology*. New York: Viking Press, 1964.

———. *The Masks of God: Oriental Mythology*. New York: Viking Penguin, 1962.

Carter, Angela. *The Bloody Chamber*. London: Penguin, 1979.

Ellmann, Mary. *Thinking About Women*. New York: Harcourt, 1968.

Ferguson, Mary Anne. *Images of Women in Literature*. Boston: Houghton Mifflin, 1973.

Fraser, Ronald. "Butor's You." *New Left Review*, May-June 1966: 62–68.

Graves, Robert. *The White Goddess*. 1948. 15th ed. New York: Farrar, Straus and Giroux, 1982.

Kolodny, Annette. "Some Notes on Defining a 'Feminist Literary Criticism.' " *Critical Inquiry* 2, 1: 75–92. Reprinted in *Feminist Criticism: Essays on Theory, Poetry and Prose*, edited by Cheryl L. Brown and Karen Olson. Metuchen: Scarecrow Press, 1978, 37–58.

Millett, Kate. *Sexual Politics*. 1969. Rpt. London: Virágo Press, 1977.

Moi, Toril. *Sexual/Textual Politics: Feminist Literary Theory*. London: Methuen, 1985.

Nochlin, Linda. "Why Have There Been No Great Women Artists?" *Art News* 69. (January 1971): 22–39.

Paglia, Camille. *Sexual Personae: Art and Decadence from Nefertiti to Emily Dickinson*. New Haven, CT: Yale University Press, 1990.

Pall, Ellen. "Starting from Scratch." *New York Times Magazine*, 24 September 1995: 39–43.

Pratt, Annis. *Archetypal Patterns in Women's Fiction*. Bloomington: Indiana University Press, 1981.

Sexton, Anne. *Transformations*. Boston: Houghton Mifflin, 1971.

Spacks, Patricia Meyer. *The Female Imagination: A Literary and Psychological Investigation of Women's Writing*. New York: Knopf, 1975.

Stubbs, Patricia. *Women and Fiction: Feminism and the Novel, 1880–1920*. 1979. Rpt. London: Methuen, 1981.

Trungpa, Chögyam. *Crazy Wisdom*. Ed. Sherab Chödzin. Boston: Shambhala, 1991.

Warner, Marina. *From the Beast to the Blonde: On Fairy Tales and Their Tellers*. New York: Farrar, Straus, and Giroux, 1994.

Woolf, Virginia. *A Room of One's Own*. New York: Harcourt Brace, 1929.

Index

About the Authors

CATHERINE E. HOYSER is Associate Professor of English at Saint Joseph College in West Hartford, Connecticut. She publishes on women, Victorian and early 20th-century literature, and detective fiction and is coeditor of *Woman: An Affirmation* (1979). She authored chapters 1 through 5 and the bibliography of this study.

LORENA LAURA STOOKEY is a lecturer in the English department at the University of Nevada, Reno, where she teaches courses in mythology, poetry, and British literature. She is the author of *Robin Cook: A Critical Companion* (Greenwood, 1996). She authored chapters 6 through 8 of this study.

**Other Titles in
Critical Companions to Popular Contemporary Writers**
Kathleen Gregory Klein, Series Editor

V. C. Andrews: A Critical Companion
E. D. Huntley

Tom Clancy: A Critical Companion
Helen S. Garson

Mary Higgins Clark: A Critical Companion
Linda C. Pelzer

Arthur C. Clarke: A Critical Companion
Robin Anne Reid

James Clavell: A Critical Companion
Gina Macdonald

Pat Conroy: A Critical Companion
Landon C. Burns

Robin Cook: A Critical Companion
Lorena Laura Stookey

Michael Crichton: A Critical Companion
Elizabeth A. Trembley

Howard Fast: A Critical Companion
Andrew Macdonald

Ken Follett: A Critical Companion
Richard C. Turner

John Grisham: A Critical Companion
Mary Beth Pringle

James Herriot: A Critical Companion
Michael J. Rossi

Tony Hillerman: A Critical Companion
John M. Reilly

John Jakes: A Critical Companion
Mary Ellen Jones

Stephen King: A Critical Companion
Sharon A. Russell

Dean Koontz: A Critical Companion
Joan G. Kotker

Anne McCaffrey: A Critical Companion
Robin Roberts

Colleen McCullough: A Critical Companion
Mary Jean DeMarr

James A. Michener: A Critical Companion
Marilyn S. Severson

Anne Rice: A Critical Companion
Jennifer Smith

John Saul: A Critical Companion
Paul Bail

Gore Vidal: A Critical Companion
Susan Baker

Erich Segal: A Critical Companion
Linda C. Pelzer